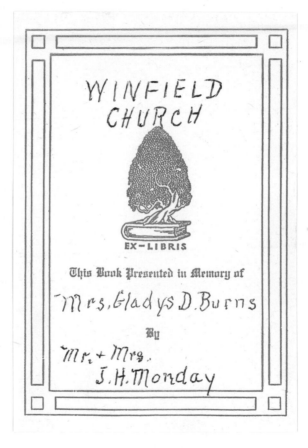

WINFIELD
CHURCH

EX-LIBRIS

This Book Presented in Memory of

Mrs. Gladys D. Burns

By

Mr. + Mrs.
J. H. Monday

Let Not Your Heart
Be Troubled

Let Not Your Heart
Be Troubled

COMFORT FOR THE BEREAVED

J. Robert Watt

Abingdon Press

NEW YORK   NASHVILLE

LET NOT YOUR HEART BE TROUBLED

Copyright © MCMLVII by Abingdon Press

Library of Congress Catalog Card Number: 57-6123

Scripture quotations designated R.S.V. are from the Revised Standard Version of the Bible and are copyright 1946 and 1952 by the Division of Christian Education of the National Council of the Churches of Christ in the U. S. A.

The poems "Peace and Joy" on p. 83 and "Patience" on pp. 24-25 are from: UNUTTERABLE BEAUTY by J. Studdert Kennedy. Copyright Harper & Brothers. Used by permission. "God's Tomorrow" on p. 53 is from: SELECTED POEMS OF JOHN OXENHAM. Copyright Harper & Brothers. Used by permission. The poem by William N. Clarke on p. 63 is from: MANY MANSIONS by John MacNeill. Copyright Harper & Brothers. Used by permission. "Prayer at the Feet of Mountains," on p. 95, is a poem from: LIGHT OF THE YEARS by Grace Noll Crowell. Copyright 1936 Harper & Brothers. Used by permission.

B

SET UP, PRINTED, AND BOUND BY THE PARTHENON PRESS, AT NASHVILLE, TENNESSEE, UNITED STATES OF AMERICA

TO

My Father and Mother

This Book Is Dedicated
in
Gratitude and Love

PREFACE

IN THE FOLLOWING PAGES NO ATTEMPT HAS BEEN MADE TO be intellectually brilliant, but rather in simple, clear words the contents are offered as a source to bring Christian comfort to those passing through the troubled waters of sorrow.

How often in our ministry we have longed for a book which might not only help the busy pastor but also be put into the hands of our people when in their hour of sorrow they come to us for comfort.

At the request of many who have been helped by these meditations, I submit them with the prayer that they might continue to bring comfort and encouragement through the spirit of the Master.

Every effort has been made to trace the authorship and to give credit for the illustrations and poems used.

At this time I should like to thank especially my wife, Verna R. M. Watt, without whose encouragement and hard work this book would not have been possible.

J. ROBERT WATT

CONTENTS

I

Piercing Death's Darkness

"There is but a step between me and death." I Sam. 20:3

THE TRAIN WAS SPEEDING THROUGH THE NIGHT. LOOKING out into the darkness one could scarcely see anything except the occasional shadow of a telegraph pole as it flashed by.

Staring rather moodily into the blackness, a passenger suddenly saw over to his left a long, clear light, cutting across the meadow. He thought, "What can it be? There's surely no highway there!" And then he realized what it was. The train was going around a curve, and the big light of his own train's engine was piercing the darkness before his very eyes. In its light the meadow seemed to come alive. He saw herds of cattle, a nearby stream, a straw pile; and then there was darkness once more as the train straightened out.

Certain words of our Bible, like the penetrating light of that super passenger train, illuminate our souls by piercing the darkness of our moods. In its beam things appear which we never dreamed were even there—the whole picture of the life we are going through takes on new meaning. Let us turn for a moment to such words as we find in I Samuel: "There is but a step between me and death."

You will all remember the story. King Saul had been

jealous of David, the shepherd. He had even sought the boy's life. On this particular day David was with his friend Jonathan, the prince. Hiding for his life, David tells his young friend that death and life are actually not very far apart and that anyone at any time might face death.

How true were the words of David! Let us look at death that we may through God's mercy understand it better.

First, what is death? Through faith in Jesus we believe that we are called through death unto life everlasting. Now, it is the things of this world that do not last. Therefore, actually it is but a step from this world and its death to the next world and its life. So often we don't look upon death in this way at all. Human in our grief, we look upon it often as the end, when the whole meaning of the Resurrection reveals it is but a step—through faith in Christ Jesus —into a beginning, a fullness of life that we can scarcely imagine.

No wonder on the Emmaus road those strong disciples hung their heads! Death had come. They believed everything was finished—until their Guest in the little dining room revealed that through death and the Cross everything was just starting. How quickly the picture changed!

Think for a moment of the artist Murillo who lived for a time in a monastery. One day he ran out of canvasses. The monks made fun of his gloom. " 'Tis the end of your painting!" they said. The cook even laughingly threw him a table napkin.

Murillo stretched it out and on it painted one of the world's great paintings: the "Madonna of the Napkin"! [1]

12

With the knowledge of what that step is, through our understanding of death, the whole picture within our souls is changed. Death is a step, not to the end, but unto life; and in so being it means something else: that we on earth are but a short distance at all times—a step, if you will—from heaven.

Think of it—but a step to those we love who have gone before! It will be a place free from the limitations of earth. A place that challenges us by its nearness to do our best—to fit our souls for the step when it comes, and in so doing to show our God that we, his highest earthly creation, can be worthy of such a place.

There in that spiritual realm will be all things wise, holy, and just. There God's purpose will prevail. As we become aware of this heavenly home, cynicism and futility are removed from within us; for we know God will be waiting to welcome, to receive, and to grant us his peace.

Isabel Cameron, in her little book *The Doctor*, tells how the minister Dr. Lindsay one day was visiting an elderly Scotsman, Donald Forsyth. He was very ill. By trade he had been a sclater (one who slates roofs) all his life, and even in this his final illness he was interested in his neighbors and their building and was wistfully wishing he could be well and back on the roof at his work once more. Now he turned to his minister and said:

I had a queer dream last nicht—I was young again, an' able for ma wark, an' I was sclating a hoose—a real bonnie hoose—an' the maister came up to see it, an' says he: "Are you near

13

dune, Donald?" "Aye," I said. "Aye, sir, twa mair sclates'll feenish," and he says: "That's richt—I'm expectin' the tenant for the hoose vera sune"—the tenant's name was written over the door, an' wha's think ye was it?

His minister didn't utter a word as the old Scotsman's eyes searched his face, but the dying man knew by his expression that he understood for he cried out triumphantly:

"Ye're richt! It was jist ma verra ain!" And he sank, happily, exhausted, upon his pillow. "That was a great dream, Donald," the doctor said softly; and then, taking his little well-worn Bible out of his pocket, he read about that house, but a step from us, "not made with hands, eternal in the heavens." [2]

> The Father's house has many rooms,
>   And each is fair;
> And some are reached through gathered glooms
>   By silent stair;
> But he keeps house, and makes it home,
> Whichever way the children come.
>
> Plenty and peace are everywhere
>   His house within;
> The rooms are eloquent with prayer,
>   The songs begin;
> And dear hearts, filled with love, are glad,
> Forgetting that they once were sad.

The Father's house is surely thine,
   Therefore why wait?
His lights of love through darkness shine,
   The hour grows late.
Push back the curtain of thy doubt,
And enter—none will cast thee out! [3]

II

Brightening the Corner

*"But go thou thy way till the end be: for thou shalt rest,
and stand in thy lot at the end of the days." Dan. 12:13*

YEARS AGO IN SUNDAY SCHOOL I USED TO WONDER, AS A
small boy, what would happen if we were to follow out
the words of that beloved hymn:

> Jesus bids us shine
>   With a pure, clear light,
> Like a little candle,
>   Burning in the night.[1]

To my childish mind there seemed to be so much darkness
in the world that a little candle would never be seen. However, as one grows older the truth of that little hymn grows
more apparent. A tiny light can be seen for a long distance
in the darkness. And a life dedicated to God creates a far
greater impression for good than we would dream of.

We can all remember loved ones who faithfully and
loyally served their church and sought, in the activity of
their lives, to make their faith real to those around them.
It wasn't always easy, yet through faith they held their
lights high. We, too, have hours of darkness. Let us for
16

a moment turn our thoughts to a verse in the book of Daniel, that the light God placed within us might continue to glow.

In Daniel's life there were many difficult problems. As in our times, there were many things that he did not understand. In his own faith, from time to time, he must have questioned God and his purpose—indeed, as we sometimes do—especially in an hour of bereavement and discouragement. He sought for truth concerning the meaning and the end of life, and one day the answer came to him: "But go thou way till the end be: for thou shalt rest, and stand in thy lot at the end of the days."

"Go back to your task, Daniel," came the voice of God to him. With his many problems he had felt himself alone in a strange and pagan land, away from his people and the burying ground of his fathers. Yet here in these words God tells Daniel not to think of death, but to go back and reveal Him in life. There was a task awaiting him.

Small though it was, it would be the task of God, and through it God would speak. Today we know that through Daniel God did speak to his people—and in our time, to us—his message of hope and comfort. Daniel's life, then, was lived as ours must be, amid small and great events; but it must be a life that ought to speak of and reflect the things of God.

A lady was standing with a group of tourists in front of the beautiful Cologne cathedral when she heard a man at her elbow say, "Didn't we do a fine piece of work there?" Turning she saw a man in plain working clothes, and speaking to him in surprise, she said, "You—what did you do about it?" The man's cheerful reply was "I mixed the mortar across the street for two years." [2]

Now, we all know that mixing mortar is one of the lesser tasks in the construction of a building. Yet what sort of buildings would there be without mortar and those who mix it? We are deeply thankful to God today for the tasks before us and for the men who face these tasks of Christian service, loyal unto the end. May we, too, be faithful, and as Ina Ogdon has put it:

> Do not wait until some deed of greatness you may do,
>   Do not wait to shed your light afar,
> To the many duties ever near you now be true,
>   Brighten the corner where you are.[3]

Now, if we are to brighten the corner where we are by loyally holding God's light high in this world's darkness, we must realize a second truth which will help us: that the end, when it comes, will be in the hands of God. We have not the capacity to grasp fully the events to come. We are not fully fit to enter into the sacredness of his understanding. Yet the Bible reveals through faith that our destinies will lie in the hands of an eternal God, who even now, through his Christ, is revealing himself day by day to us.

E. Stanley Jones once told of how a Mohammedan taunted an Indian Christian with the fact that Mohammedans had a tomb of the prophet where they could worship, but the Christians were not even sure where

18

Jesus was buried. Quickly came back the Christian's reply: "We have no certain tomb because we have no corpse." [4] How right he was! It is the living Christ in life and death who can lead us into the future which has been prepared for those who are worthy.

Not only, then, was Daniel told to carry on, that the future was in God's hands, but that in that future there would be a place for him. Insofar as we are faithful and true, there'll be a place for us where loved ones will be waiting and where we shall be ruled over by a God whom, through Jesus, we already know. When our bodies fail and spirits flag, we'll not need to fear the coming of the shadow of death, but trustingly we can step forward to our higher home above.

For years a steamboat company ran a pleasure cruise up the Magnetawan River in northern Ontario. It lasted a whole day. During the day the people on board the boat passed a number of camps and villages dotting the river bank. Finally, at the end of the day as the boat was returning, they came to the high point of their cruise; for in the gathering dusk they beheld the lights of their own town. It was different from all the other villages they had seen, for it was home, and after a long trip it was good to be coming home.

Loved ones also rejoice to return to that heavenly home, and we pray God that some day we, too, in the gathering dusk shall behold its lights.

> Somewhere beyond—I know not where,
> Beneath what fair unclouded skies;

I only know beyond—somewhere,
The Land of Fulfilled Promise lies.

I hear the call, I see the light—
A sure clear gleam upon the way;
And up the steep, across the night,
I go to meet the certain Day.[5]

III

Returning Goodness

"And of his fulness have all we received, and grace for grace."   John 1:16

RECENTLY A FRIEND WHO LIVES IN A VERY LARGE CITY came to visit us in our summer cottage. The chief topic of conversation in the city where he lives was the shortage of water. It had not rained for over a month. The lawns were brown, and water was rationed. As he stood looking out over the seemingly limitless waters of Lake Huron, he said, "At last, here is a place where there is no shortage of water."

When we stop to think, we realize there are many blessings of God which are unlimited. How we take them for granted! John, in his Gospel, spoke of this when he said: "And of his fulness have all we received, and grace for grace." For instance, we can think of the fresh clean air we breathe, of the warmth of the morning sun that drives back the cool air of the night, of the craving and desire for better things within us, and of the way God has created the world to answer this craving. No matter how often you smell a rose, there is always perfume left; no matter how long you gaze at a sunset, its beauty goes on undiminished.

> There's enough of God
> In the heart of a rose,
> In the smile of a child,
> In the dewy blossom of dawn
>   To prove
> That beauty is the soul of Him,
> That Love is His sceptre,
> And that all things created by Him,
> Face not the night
> But an eternal morning.[1]

These physical things for which we are thankful, in the above words of the poet, remind us there is something even finer. For just as God has bestowed upon us so many earthly blessings, we realize that he has bestowed many spiritual blessings upon us as well. These are blessings which can comfort and strengthen us.

The Bible says: "Of his fulness have all we received." Consciously or unconsciously, everyone shares in the grace of the Lord Jesus.

Out of his wondrous goodness to us Jesus has revealed what immortal life would be like. With the simplicity which he always used in his dealing with the great things of the gospel, he set forth his idea of what awaited God's people after their days on this earth would be done. There would be a home. God would be there. For those of faith it would be a place of love and happiness. There is not much detail here. How simply his belief is put forth! But it is sufficient. This is the picture that ought to come to our hearts and souls when we share in the sorrow of

22

death. For it is a true picture, and there comes from it comfort and courage to raise our eyes, as our loved ones would have us do, and to go on living in the same spirit and with the same faith.

Paul points out that out of the fullness of God comes his grace. Can we ever define what the grace of God can do for us? For in the fullness of his grace, not only is there comfort stemming from the fact that we know where our loved ones have gone, but there is comfort when we realize that the love which created eternity is even now within our reach to help us be eternal, by the way we face life's purposes.

Somebody once said, "Life is full of tension." Is not tension created out of a clash of purpose, and fear of the outcome? The question before us is—are we fulfilling the purpose of God? Before we can fulfill it, we must be aware of it. Then tension will be replaced by an urgency to serve lovingly, and to be at our best. When we do this, not tension, but peace of soul, can and will be the result in our hearts. We shall then not only be partakers of his grace but also be transmitters of it to the world, as we share his purpose and spirit with others. Then someday, we like our loved ones who have gone before us, will be ready for heaven.

Most of us as children were reared on the exciting stories of the famous Wilfred T. Grenfell. You will recall that he left a highly successful medical practice in London, England, to bring healing to the uncared-for people of Labrador. Here he was called one day to minister to a fisherman who was critically ill. The choice before him was this:

would he go around the point which would be the safest route, or would he cut across the ice on the bay, saving many precious hours?

He decided that though the ice was soft, he would risk cutting across the bay. Halfway across, he heard an ominous crack. The ice was beginning to break up. In a matter of minutes he found himself on an ice floe, drifting helplessly out to sea. He knew almost certain death awaited him. One by one he called his dogs to him and mercifully killed them. He fashioned from their hides a fur covering and erected a little mast from which a piece of cloth fluttered. Then he calmly went to sleep.

After some time the ice floe was seen and the good doctor was rescued. Later he was asked how it was possible for him to sleep under such circumstances, and he said simply, "I had done all I could do—the rest lay in God's hands. Of what was there to be afraid?"

Here was the faith of a man who daily shared God's purposes in life. As he received of God's grace, he attempted in his own way to pass it on, and so can we. In each round of daily duties we can reveal the faith that is within us and so bring honor and glory unto our Lord. We thank God then that out of his goodness he has called us unto himself, taking away the darkness of death, allowing us to serve him while living, and repaying—in part, at least—his goodness to us.

> Sometimes I wish that I might do
> Just one grand deed and die,

And by that one grand deed reach up
   To meet God in the sky.

But such is not Thy way, O God,
   Not such is Thy decree,
But deed by deed, and tear by tear,
   Our souls must climb to Thee.[2]

IV

Fear Not

"And it was now dark, and Jesus was not come to them."
John 6:17

WE ALL HAVE MOMENTS OF DARKNESS, MOMENTS WHEN
cold, biting fear gnaws into our souls and we see no way
out of the situation which has come upon us. It's like
being caught in a vise from which there is no release.
Many things can cause this. Failure on our part, disappointment in friends who let us down, or death—each can
bring darkness to our souls.

The Bible tells us of a group of men who one day felt
this loneliness so deeply that they had to have outside
help. It's an old story, yet how vivid was their need!

Late in the day, the disciples had set out across the Sea
of Galilee while Jesus went up to a nearby hill to pray. As
often happens a storm arose, and the little boat and its
crew were soon in difficulty.

After a while the Master arose from his knees and,
looking out across the water, saw their plight. Realizing
their need, he went to them across the water.

With cracked and bleeding hands they labored. Their
backs ached. They were about ready to give up when they
saw him. Not knowing who he was, they were afraid
until, above the storm, in spite of all its fierceness, they

heard his voice: "Be of good cheer—it is I—be not afraid."

They didn't recognize Jesus at first, for the Bible says that he would have passed them by. They didn't recognize him because he did not come as they expected he would come. There was no blare of heavenly trumpets. The sky did not open with a blaze of flashing glory—he simply appeared, walking on the water by their side. How like the disciples we are! In our own time we would have expected the Lord to have simply said a word from shore. Or we would have hunted for a magic button so that we could have summoned him quickly to our side. It wasn't needed then. It's not needed now! He knows us: who we are, where we are, and how we are. What is necessary is that we raise our eyes, so that we, too, can behold our Saviour and in spirit know that he is with us. For he comes to us, especially in an hour of trial.

> One there lives, whose guardian eye
> Guides our humble destiny;
> One there lives, who, Lord of all,
> Keeps our feathers lest they fall.
>
> Pass we blithely then the time,
> Fearless of the snare and lime,
> Free from doubt and faithless sorrow:
> God provideth for the morrow.[1]

The Scriptures reveal that Jesus came during the fourth watch at dawn. He came to them when their spirits were at their lowest ebb—it was an hour of their greatest need.

In like manner he comes to us, and with him comes the dawn. For no matter how great our disappointment or bereavement, he reveals that there is life to be lived and eternity to be won and cultivated within our souls. He points out that there is a task to do, and he will watch over us as we do it. After all, nothing could have happened to that little group. They were his band! They were being trained for a part in God's revelation to man. There would come a time, it is true, when they would face death—but the arms of an everlasting God would take them unto himself when that time came.

There is an old legend told of Michelangelo. One day he was busy on a painting. He grew tired and fell asleep at his work. While he slept an angel came and, seizing the brush from the sleeping artist's fingers, finished the picture. After a while Michelangelo wakened and looked at his canvas; his heart was thrilled with what he saw! Somehow, his picture had been completed by a hand far more skilled than his. Something of the light, and touch, of God seemed to glow from it.[2] Michelangelo had done his best, and according to the legend, God had done the rest.

In it all he perceived that God had been watching over him and he had not been alone. God had been aware of the artist's tiredness and shortcomings and in His own way had sent him on, encouraged to do better work.

May the knowledge of God's presence with us and his watching care over us lift us out of the doldrums of any despair into which we might fall and send us forth as his band, into life and living.

White Captain of my soul, lead on;
I follow Thee, come dark or dawn.
Only vouchsafe three things I crave:
Where terror stalks, help me be brave!
Where righteous ones can scarce endure
The siren call, help me be pure!
Where vows grow dim, and men dare do
What once they scorned, help me be true.[3]

V

The Rock

"The Lord is my rock, and my fortress." Ps. 18:2

PICTURE FOR A MOMENT A WIND-SWEPT, TREELESS DESERT.
The burning sun beats down upon the sand. Upon its
bosom, we see a distant speck, a weary, exhausted traveler,
slowly making his way.

Away in the distance he can see a great rock, and in his
imagination he can feel the cool of its shade and taste
already, upon his parched tongue, the water of a nearby
stream. As he views the rock in the distance, the traveler
takes fresh courage. Now he does not want to give up,
and he presses on so that in reality he can share in the good
things that he knows will be found at its base.

It is a beautiful picture of hope, and our lives can benefit
from its message to us. The psalmist found that the Lord
was his rock, and as he looked to Him a new spirit seemed
to enter within him, new purpose and hope lay before him,
and he pressed, as Paul said, "on toward the goal for the
prize of the upward call of God" (R.S.V.), knowing that
God was there to sustain and help him.

In our cynical, modern minds, however, we find it hard
to believe, don't we, that the Lord is even aware of our
stumblings over the hot sands of life's deserts, to say
nothing of watching for us to help us and to lift us up?

30

Some years ago Viscount Gray of England visited Harvard University. In a little informal talk to the students he told them that when he served in the Foreign Office in London they received word that President Theodore Roosevelt intended to visit them. President Roosevelt had been traveling through Africa and Europe, and he stated that he was planning his holiday in such a way that he might visit England in the spring, when the birds would be in full song.

He was met at Waterloo Station. He spent a number of days around the little country village of Titchborne. Viscount Gray said:

I found that Colonel Roosevelt had a remarkable interest in birds . . . . If three or four birds were singing together he would pick out their songs, distinguish each, and ask to be told each separate name. . . .

Once we were passing under a fir tree when we heard a small song in the tree above us. As we stopped I said that was the song of a golden-crested wren. . . . Then he said, "I think that is exactly the same as the song of a bird we have in America."

Later, relating this incident to a bird expert in the Natural History Museum in London, the specialist said that Roosevelt was right, that the song of this bird was the only song those two countries had in common.[1]

Imagine a man—a busy man like Roosevelt—being able to pick out, among thousands of birds of America and Europe, the one bird which had a similar song back home!

31

If a man can do that, how much more can God do! Jesus said that God was aware of even a sparrow when it fell. How much more would he be conscious of those created in his own image! He is aware of us, and because he loves us he yearns to receive us. There he stands in our midst, revealing that a new purpose and hope lies before us because through the Cross we are all his children—children of hope!

> In hope that sends a shining ray
> Far down the future's broadening way;
> In peace that only Thou canst give,
> With Thee, O Master, let me live.[2]

Not only is the rock a symbol of hope toward which we move, but it's something on which we can depend; it's enduring!

The rock, for the traveler, was a permanent feature of the landscape. The travelers all knew that beyond the heat of the desert they could count on the rock's being there with its shade and spring of cold water. It never changed!

God is always the same—yesterday, today, and tomorrow. As we face these things in human life that darken our skies and trouble us, we know and we believe that just as God has helped us in the past, he will be our stay and refuge in the present.

When Alexander the Great marched to conquer Persia, barriers of snow and ice wore down his soldiers. Legend has it that they became discouraged and filled with the futility of their progress, and they refused to go any farther.

Seeing this, Alexander rode up; he himself got down from his horse and began to hack away at the ice. The men stared in amazement and with renewed interest. Their leader was with them! One by one they got to their feet again and hacked their way with him through the frozen barrier to victory.

The rock is a symbol of One who endures to the end —of One who is with us, helping us to accomplish that which we could not do ourselves; and through faith we believe that end will be in God. This leads us to our final thought.

The rock reminds us that there is more to life than the sands of the desert. We are not simply travelers of the desert lands of human experiences, for we are spiritual travelers, and as a result we draw on spiritual resources!

In the center of our earthly impoverishment, when we're least likely to expect it, we can draw deeply of the power of God, which will enable us to endure to the end and by which we can see a meaning to these things which happen to us.

On a dusty road the artist Gibson walked one day with a friend. The artist stated there was beauty in everything; his friend disagreed. "Look," he said, "at the dirty, dusty road in front of us. Can you see God and his beauty there?" Gibson thoughtfully walked on a little; then, stooping down, he picked up a dried, curled, dust-covered leaf. Slowly his fingers opened it, and both men saw inside a tiny bug, beautifully colored.

Yes, even on life's dusty, terrifying, lonely roads we find

Him. His strength is sufficient for our needs, for like the psalmist, we, too, shall find: "The Lord is my rock and my fortress!"

> My hope is built on nothing less
> Than Jesus' blood and righteousness;
> I dare not trust the sweetest frame,
> But wholly lean on Jesus' name.
>
> When darkness veils His lovely face
> I rest on His unchanging grace;
> In every high and stormy gale,
> My anchor holds within the veil.
>
> On Christ, the solid rock, I stand;
> All other ground is sinking sand.[3]

VI

Always Moving

"For what is your life?" Jas. 4:14

WHEN WE COMMIT OUR LOVED ONES UNTO GOD, LET US realize that it isn't simply an act of memory, but an act whereby we renew our faith in God. Though we do not understand all that takes place, yet, through Jesus Christ our Lord, we do believe that what takes place is best and that it can contribute further to our understanding of God's will.

We ought not spiritually ever to stand still. Each experience in life should contribute to our spiritual stature. The hour of sorrow is no exception, for as loved ones are taken from us, we realize that life itself is not a stationary thing.

How often we have stood upon a bridge and watched a piece of floating bark move gently with the current, down the stream! How often we have seen a ball of wastepaper go down the street, blown by the wind until it, too, disappears from view! How like life! Through babyhood, childhood, and adulthood we go, and the years seem to fly! The older we get, the faster they fly, and there's continual change around us.

In a spiritual sense this, too, is true. As we trust the Lord and face these experiences of life, our faith deepens,

35

and we move toward a deeper understanding of God and his purpose. Unlike the piece of bark floating down the stream with no real destination, we believe we have a goal. We are advancing toward it, hour by hour, day by day, in the care and love of our heavenly Father.

Surely the knowledge of God's presence with us and heaven before us, and the fact that we are part of his church and fellowship, on earth and in heaven, ought to bring a sense of peace and joy unto us!

In his *Studies in the Gospel of John,* George Eckman tells of a minister, Newman Hall by name, who arrived one day on the summit of Snowdon Mountain in Wales. He arrived as the men were gathering around the quarry mouth, and when they heard he was a minister of God, they asked him to speak.

Only a few of the miners could speak English, so Newman Hall said, "I'll not preach a sermon—but I will pray." He held up his hands for silence. The men removed their caps. The minister, by the open pit of the mine, raised his voice in prayer.

Two years went by. One day, in another part of England, Newman Hall was stopped by a stranger who said, "You'll not know me, sir, but I remember you! You offered a prayer one day by a mine pit in the heart of Wales, did you not?"

"Why, yes," said the surprised minister, "but I remember very few of you could speak English. Why, I didn't think you'd understand a word, let alone remember about it!"

"That's correct," said the miner, "most of us did speak only the Welsh, but we knew what you were doing. We

36

knew to Whom you were praying. We all felt something of his presence binding us together. In fact, our village has never been the same since! In our area alone, fifty men who before never darkened a church doorway gave their hearts to God. And for them I should like to say 'thanks' today." Newman Hall could only shake the man's hand in good-bye—he was left speechless.

It had been a most unusual place to pray, at the mouth of a dark mine shaft, especially to men who could not understand his words; yet God had been there! [1]

It might even appear to some a most unusual place to speak of joy in the midst of grief, yet, because God is always present, there does come his peace and inward serenity to our souls. For we realize that not only does he sustain us, but he points the direction toward which our lives are moving and toward which our loved ones have gone.

Our lives, through faith in the Master of all men, can be the outward, working projection of divine purpose and thought. God, in us, moves to meet and to overcome the evil of our world. In the ensuing struggle our souls are fashioned and strengthened. We are gripped by a grasp that will not let us go. And when our time comes to join those we love, as we enter the valley of the shadow, we, too, shall find that it will be a love that will continue to hold us and lead us to life eternal.

> O Love that wilt not let me go,
> I rest my weary soul in Thee;
> I give Thee back the life I owe,
> That in Thine ocean depths its flow

May richer, fuller be.

. . . .

O Cross that liftest up my head,
I dare not ask to fly from Thee;
I lay in dust life's glory dead,
And from the ground there blossoms red
Life that shall endless be.[2]

Men might block his plans, yet above the power of
man is eternal God. His alternate purpose will be fulfilled.
Through the dark days of the Cross, Christ marched
triumphantly forward, gripped by the eternal vision before
him. He faced and conquered death—that we might live.
Why, then, should we fear death? Why should we doubt?

Thackeray, in his *Newcomes,* tells about the old Colonel,
the headmaster of the school. He was very ill. The chapel
bell began to peal. The old man heard it, and his hands
outside the bed covers tried feebly to keep the beats of the
tune. Just as the last bell struck, a sweet smile lit up his
face; and lifting his head a little, he said, as though he
heard his name being called on a far-away roll: "Adsum"—
present!

We thank God today for a place where, when he's ready,
we shall hear our names called and we shall rise, as our
loved ones have, through a faith that is always moving
and growing unto the joy of our Lord and his home for us.

Thou, who hast made my home of life so pleasant,
    Leave not its tenant when its walls decay:
O Love Divine, O Helper ever present,
    Be Thou my strength and stay! [3]

38

VII

Living On

"If a man die, shall he live again?" Job 14:14

CLARENCE E. MACARTNEY, IN ONE OF HIS BOOKS, TELLS OF an American who was walking up a hill in Norway. He grew tired about halfway up the path and stopped for a rest. Down below him was the valley, and as he looked out upon the scene below, he saw something that made him reach immediately to remove his hat.

There in the little village beneath, he saw men emerging out of a cottage, carrying with them a rude coffin. It was placed on a wagon, and then the little procession wound up the road and across a new-mown hayfield to the churchyard.

For a short while there was a silence as the service proceeded, like a sabbath silence over the fields. The little company then broke up, going their several ways, each waiting his time until for him life's little episode would be over. Slowly the church bell began to toll, and slowly the American put his hat back on. He thought, as he did so, of the question that is often in the minds of people and is found in the scripture: "If a man die, shall he live again?" As he began to climb again, he was thankful for his belief in God.[1]

What about our belief in God? We, too, time and time again, are faced with the same question, and the answer to

39

our souls comes from the very lips of Jesus himself. "Whosoever believeth in him should not perish, but have everlasting life." For our encouragement and comfort let us look at certain ways in which we can live on.

First of all, we live on in memories. Everyone can think of people whose thoughts and actions have influenced them. It may be a Sunday-school teacher of whom we think, or a parent, or a day-school teacher; and in so doing we realize that one of God's greatest gifts to us is the gift of memory.

Some years ago when we were on vacation, a tiny white-haired old lady stopped in to visit for a little with us. She had been my eighth-grade teacher. Almost wistfully, she mentioned that she had now retired and that she hoped through her teaching she had done some good.

As I sat there, it was easy to imagine myself once more in the class. She was one of the finest eighth-grade teachers it was possible for anyone to have had. Each year she had some thirty to forty students to teach. None could, or would, ever forget her and the training she gave. How memory retains the things of those we love, especially those who have helped us.

Each of us also lives on in our influence. Be it good, bad, or indifferent, each of us adds to the things that shape our world. What an opportunity for us then as Christian people! John Greenleaf Whittier once wrote:

> From scheme and creed the light goes out,
>   The saintly fact survives;
> The blessed Master none can doubt
>   Revealed in holy lives.[2]

Standing one day on Hamilton Mountain overlooking the town of Grimsby, Ontario, a young person once remarked as he pointed, "There's where I live." It was a beautiful view, and though we were admiring it, most of us were more concerned, like that young person was, with trying to find the house in which we lived. Is not this a parable for us all? God grants to us visions—high moments of inspiration to take back down into the valleys and on to the streets where we live. The question, then, is whether we are true to the vision he gives us, or whether we are concerned with self alone, and the particular place where we live in life? How we answer this question will determine whether our influence on those around us is good or bad!

Yes, we live on in memories, we live on in our influence on others, and there is something still further; for through faith in Jesus Christ we shall someday live on in eternity.

If I were to visit some of you folk who like gardening, or go to a florist's shop and ask to see down in the cellar, I should find there during the winter months rows and rows of flower pots. You would explain to me that they contain bulbs and that it is best for winter bulbs to be rooted in the dark in order to prepare them for the light a little later on.

Can we not in a similar way picture in the turmoil and the darkness of this world's problems, a God, cultivating and developing our souls, allowing them to be growing toward the light, so that when death comes we shall be prepared for the possibilities which God in heaven has prepared for us?

Once a devout old man was very ill. He was asked by his closest friend, "Do you expect to go to heaven?" The sick man thought for a little, and his face lit up as he said, "Man! I live there!" Through his faith in Jesus he grasped the great truth of God. It was the truth that not someday, but now, the soul can lay hold of immortality; and we recognize then, for a Christian, that death is but the passing from this life into something infinitely greater, beyond.

"If a man die, shall he live again?"—Let us hear again His words in answer: "He that believeth on me hath everlasting life."

> There is no death! What seems so is transition.
>   This life of mortal breath
> Is but a suburb of the life elysian,
>   Whose portal we call Death.[3]

VIII

Never Alone

"I will not fail thee, nor forsake thee." Josh. 1:5

SADNESS WAS HANGING OVER THE VALLEYS OF ISRAEL. Word had just come that their great leader Moses was dead. God had called him. In subdued tones throughout the tents the elders, down to the children, were discussing this thing that had happened. We can imagine their feelings, can't we? Their civic leader, their spiritual counselor, the one to whom they turned to for this and for that, was no more. What would they do? And, in particular, the young Joshua was downcast.

Suddenly, in the midst of his mourning, the voice of God spoke to him: "As I was with Moses, so I will be with thee: I will not fail thee, nor forsake thee. . . . Only be thou strong and very courageous, that thou mayest observe to do according to all the law."

There are times in our lives when we would do well to hear the voice of God within our souls, as he spoke that day to Joshua: "I will not fail thee, nor forsake thee."

Human friends might fail us. We often fail ourselves, don't we, by attempting to leave our better selves behind; but God will never fail us. For here in these words is revealed the unalterable truth that the One who can give us life everlasting is always by our side, and on him we can depend.

There is a story told of a king who sent wise men to bring him a motto which would serve for good days or bad. Finally they came back, and the choice was made; it was —"This too shall pass away." [1]

Surely it is a good slogan for us all to remember. It teaches us to appreciate, while life's sky is sunny, the happiness that can be ours; and then when clouds loom and there is sadness, it teaches us that this, too, is a part of life—a part God shares with us, and as we realize that he is with us, we know it, too, shall pass.

Now, God does not fail us, because he never gives us up! We are his children. You would never give your child up as long as you were able, in any way, to help him and to contribute to his happiness, would you? No more would God! Even in the most difficult and exasperating attitudes of life, our heavenly Father seeks to reconcile his children of earth unto himself. We are his. Through the Cross he has bought us with a price. Sons and daughters of God, through Jesus—no wonder he will not give us up!

William Stidger once heard Parkes Cadman tell of a boyhood incident. Parkes had been working in a coal mine. His job was to drive the mule, pulling small loaded coal cars along the darkened tunnel, across a dangerous intersection, and out to be unloaded. At this intersection a number of boys had been killed with runaway cars; Parkes had heard about this. It was his first try. He was afraid, terribly so, as he approached that crossing in the darkness. Then "he saw a tiny gleam of light, and when he reached the intersection he brushed a tear from his eyes with his dirty sleeve, making a smear down across his cheeks. He

44

smiled as he looked up through the mist in his tear-filled eyes, for there stood his own father, a coal miner, with a lantern in his hands. He had thought of the boy's danger and fears as he made his first approach to that intersection." [2]

At his most difficult place his father had stood, ready to help him. At the intersection of human living that all of us sooner or later come to, there is our God—"our refuge and strength in time of trouble."

One day to the parsonage door there came a man. After being admitted into the hall, he stood for a moment, as though searching for the right words to say. His minister waited. Then he said simply, "Thanks for everything— I'm moving this week." The minister looked at him, searching his mind for anything he had done to help this man. He could think of nothing. He told his parishioner so, and the answer he received was one he could never forget, for the man said simply, "You were always there if I needed you. It helped me so much to know that. If ever I had needed to knock on your door, you would have opened it to me."

As we commit a loved one unto the care of God, we know that God will hear his tap upon the door, and his faith and trust in his Father will be fulfilled. Let us now rise, like Joshua, to the task at hand—to do His will and to serve Him better, knowing: "I will not fail thee, nor forsake thee."

I know not when I go or where
From this familiar scene;

45

But He is here and He is there,
  And all the way between;
And when I leave this life I know,
  For that dim vast unknown,
Though late I stay, or soon I go,
  I shall not go alone.[3]

IX

Moving Toward the Fold

"Mine age is departed, and is removed from me as a shepherd's tent."   Isa. 38:12

HERE IS A PICTURE TAKEN FROM OUR BIBLE, AND A VERY common one in Eastern lands. It is the picture of shepherds building temporary huts. They have gathered available branches, and quickly they set up lean-tos that will protect them from the bitter night winds. Some shepherds even carry their black skin tents with them, erecting them near their grazing sheep.

The sheep soon eat up the grass, and after a few weeks the flocks are moved on. Once more the tents are taken down, or if huts have been used, they are simply discarded until a new pasture is found and new lean-tos built.

Isaiah, in these words, is comparing our life to such a picture. We pitch our tents in various places, but none are permanent until God calls us. The hymn writer James Montgomery had the same thought when he wrote:

> "For ever with the Lord!"
>   Amen! so let it be!
> Life from the dead is in that word,
>   'Tis immortality.
>
> Here in the body pent,
>   Absent from Him I roam,

> Yet nightly pitch my moving tent
> A day's march nearer home.[1]

Time and time again, we all feel the cold, biting feeling of insecurity. A friend is with us one moment, and then he is gone. We build our lives on certain plans; in a matter of seconds they can come crumbling down around our ears! Life seems to consist of a series of shifting scenes. Yet, in spite of the temporary nature of this life, there are certain things we can grasp and hold on to and be sure of— things unlike the shepherd's tents—things which don't move and on which we can count. Especially is this true when loved ones are called from us.

One of these things is the fact that God seeks to use us in life and therefore has a purpose for us.

It has been my privilege, from time to time, to speak over radio station CKNX, Wingham, Ontario, during their morning devotional period. One day a letter came from a man down near Windsor, over two hundred miles away. He has a little radio in his barn. He listens to it while he does his chores. On this particular morning he had been forking hay while listening to the broadcast; then, in his own words: "I set down the fork, for I heard a new and startling thought—to think that God could use me and has a purpose for me—why, it could change my whole attitude to life!" There he was, standing between the cattle stalls; and as he listened there was opened up by the Holy Spirit, through those words, a new glimpse of eternal realities all about him and his part in connection with them. Isaiah sensed this, too. Though the things around him changed

48

and decayed, yet the things of God endured. He was aware of them. It influenced him.

Now, as we dwell on these things of God, it does not mean we should forget or let up on our earthly duties; rather, it ought to stimulate us to serve, on earth, the true things that will abide forever. It will give new direction to these duties, and to us, a new understanding of them as we perform them.

Jenny Lind rather suddenly retired from a famous career, and one day shortly afterward a friend found her sitting on a deserted seashore. She was leaning against a stone and looking out across the water to watch the sun go down. A Bible was lying open upon her lap.

After a little her friend asked her, "Why did you give up your career, Jenny?"

She smiled, "Because," she said, "I had discovered that every stage I crossed, every roar of applause I heard, made me think less of that," and she nodded at the sunset, "and never of this," and she glanced down at her Bible.[2] She refused to continue to let the temporary things of life destroy the real person she was capable of being!

Each of us, too, as we fulfill God's purpose, enters into the reality of things that endure, which leads us to grasp the next truth which never changes; because of this each of us has hope of life everlasting.

As we come to the end of life we find, like our loved ones before us have found, that we are not the shepherds, but rather the sheep of the Good Shepherd! The Shepherd knows his sheep; he will find our hands and lead us not into the folds that change, which are dependent upon how the winds blow or whether rain has fallen, but into the folds which are sustained by the love and grace of the everlasting God.

Just as serving God in life changes the whole meaning of life, so does this understanding of death change the attitude of our sorrow. We realize we are children not only of this shifting world but also of the world that is to be. We need not hate it! We need not fear it!

A minister was called one day to visit an old man who was very ill. They were good friends. The old man's lot had been hard, but he had been faithful. He said, "I'm ready now. I've done my best to live out God's purpose on earth. I know God will fulfill his purpose for me in heaven." Such ought to be our faith!

We therefore offer a prayer of thanks to God for these things that do not change and for the good Shepherd who, in life or death, will lead us into the fold everlasting.

> The Shepherd does not ask of thee
>   Faith in thy faith, but only faith in Him:
> And this He meant in saying, "come to me."
>   In light or darkness, seek to do His will,
>   And leave the work of faith to Jesus still.[3]

X

The Darkened Doorway

"I am the resurrection, and the life: he that believeth in me, though he were dead, yet shall he live." John 11:25

OUR THOUGHTS TURN FOR A MOMENT TO A LITTLE VILLAGE lying at the outskirts of the great city of Jerusalem. It is the village of Bethany, and as we enter it we see a band of dusty travelers approaching a certain cottage. As they make their way up the pathway, they are greeted by an older sister of the household, who rushes out to meet them —Martha!

We hear her cry, "Lord, if thou hadst been here, my brother had not died." Then the gentle voice of the Master is heard as he says, "Thy brother shall live again!" And then there fell from the lips of Jesus those wonderful words: "I am the resurrection, and the life: he that believeth in me, though he were dead, yet shall he live: And whosoever liveth and believeth in me shall never die."

It is in the spirit of these great words that we can come under the shadow of death and commit our loved ones unto the care of God. Though we shall miss our loved ones, and though someone is going to have to volunteer to carry on the work of God that they so faithfully did, yet in our hearts there is a deep thankfulness to God for their faith and for the promise revealed in those wonderful words of

Jesus: "That whosoever believeth in me shall not die, but have everlasting life."

One Sunday I was asked to take an evening anniversary service in a tiny village. I arrived a few moments before the service was to start. It was dark, and very few lights seemed to be on. I asked a man whom I met where the church was, and he said, "I will take you to it." He led me down the street to a long, low building, the exterior of which was in darkness. The church actually was not quite completed, and as yet no lights had been installed outside. Unaware of this at the time, I thought to myself, "What a dismal place! No light outside, and there'll probably be nobody inside!" As the man opened the door, however, light from the inside blazed out into the darkness. The church was filled with people waiting for me, and I found them to be friendly and happy. How often the doorway of death looks gloomy and dark from where we stand in this earthly life, hampered by our human limitations. Still, if these words of Jesus are true, and we believe they are, then what a change will await our loved ones as they are led through the darkened doorway of death to the light, the happiness, the loving friends within.

This brings comfort to us, and ought also to help us see that life has greater dimensions than would appear on the surface. It means putting a plus quality into life, for we are children with a destiny. We move, we act, we think, we say—all under the watchful gaze of God and the eyes of our loved ones in heaven.

Sylvester Horne, according to William Stidger, was a much-beloved teacher in a small American college. Quite often in his classes he spoke to the students of certain high thoughts which came to him while walking in his garden. One night certain of his students were invited to his home for tea. After supper they asked if they might see his garden, for he had spoken so often of it, and so many great thoughts had seemingly come to him while he was there. When they saw it they could only stare. It was so plain and very, very ordinary; and there was altogether only a few square feet of grass. One of the boys exclaimed, "Your garden, sir, it's so small—" Dr. Horne smiled as he looked at their surprised faces and said, "Yes, it is very tiny, but see how high it goes." And the students realized that it was not outward, but upward, that his thoughts went.[1] May God grant to us that upward look, that we, in our sorrow and hardships, might perceive eternity beyond this life, and that for us some day, as well as for our loved ones, the words of Jesus might be fulfilled. "He that believeth in me, though he were dead, yet shall he live."

> The night is very black and grim,
> —Our hearts are sick with sorrow,—
> But, on the rim of the curtain dim,
> A pulsing beam, a tiny gleam,
> Whispers of God's To-morrow.
>
> Beyond the night there shines a light
> —Our eyes are dim with sorrow,—
> But Faith still clings, and Hope still springs,
> And Love still sings of happier things,
> For life is flighting strong new wings
> In search of God's To-morrow.[2]

XI

By My Side

"The Lord stood with me, and strengthened me."
II Tim. 4:17

WHEN A FAITHFUL SERVANT OF THE MASTER IS CALLED
to the higher service, we sense our loss and feel our need
of outside strength.

Paul, too, faced difficult moments, yet he found there
was a strength to help him. In Second Timothy he wrote:
"The Lord stood with me, and strengthened me."

In recent years we in America have been experiencing
hurricanes. We've named them Hazel, Connie, and Diane.
These names are no indication of their natures, for they
have left widespread havoc in their wakes. One thing we
seldom have, however, is an earthquake. Some nations do
have them, and they're quite severe.

A missionary home from Japan tells of two little Japanese
girls of Tokyo who were comparing experiences one day
after such an earthquake. One had gone with her parents
to the Buddhist temple, where immense throngs, silent
and helpless, had passed before the idols. "Our parents
just looked at the gods and scowled," said one child. The
other little girl had attended a service led by the Christian
missionary, and she replied, "Our people looked up to
God and sang and began to build their homes again."

In our world today we see many pillars of our civiliza-

54

tion tilting and cracking. In our lives we find problems. Suddenly, in an hour of unexpected bereavement, we face grief. Still, in it all, we are not bowed down. Through faith we can raise our eyes upward and acknowledge God's goodness, for "He is with us, and He will strengthen us."

If I were to stop certain people on the street and ask them what they would like most of all, some would say health; others, wealth; still others, position, peace—and perhaps a few would say "a greater consciousness of God." Could there be a greater gift than these? Yes, there is; surely one of the greatest gifts that God has given to us is simply the knowledge that whether it be a happy or a sorrowing time, he is here to help us.

The apostle Paul had physical affliction. In his heart lay the cold loneliness of being separated from loved ones. He had felt the weight of human blundering. In Nero's prison, just before his death, he penned these words of personal faith and tested power. They came from the melting fires of his suffering. "The Lord stood with me, and strengthened me." It is at such a point in our own lives where we must look above the immediate affliction and respond to God's presence in the fulfillment of his purpose still before us in life.

It was only on the Damascus road that Paul, confronted by the Christ, looked up and saw himself and what, with God's power, he might do. It was for that purpose that Jesus came: to bring us into a living consciousness of the God that created us. In so doing we can be grasped by a power that could lift us up out of the flatlands of our grief into new levels of service. It can do more than this for us!

For when we realize that part of our family is now in heaven, it means that we can be our family's representative of God here on earth.

John Ruskin, who was very fond of art, argued that no artist or creative worker could ever do his best work if he confined himself only to the representation of human achievements. He must represent the work of God—the flowers, the fields, the trees. Archer Wallace points out that if this is true, then is it unreasonable to assume that we must imitate the Divine to give our best? I would go further.

As we recognize God's presence here to help us, we must also recognize it is a call to place our wills and personalities at the disposal of God's will and personality. Then we will love truth more than triumph, honesty more than honors; and God, as he did for our loved ones, will shape our souls and can use us for the betterment of our community and of our world.

In the many little stories told of Tennyson, there is one which tells that one day in a beautiful flower garden he was walking with a friend. His friend said to him, "Mr. Tennyson, you speak so often of Jesus; will you tell me what Christ means to your life?" Tennyson stopped, and pointing down to a beautiful yellow flower, he said, "What the sun is to that flower, Christ is to my soul." Beauty was there in that flower because it had responded to the light and warmth of God's sun above.

We thank God for loved ones everywhere who did respond to the finer things of life, and may we, as God's strength and spirit lift us up, dedicate ourselves anew to his service.

> I go to prove my soul!
> I see my way as birds their trackless way.
> I shall arrive! what time, what circuit first,
> I ask not: but unless God send his hail
> Or blinding fireballs, sleet or stifling snow,
> In some time, his good time, I shall arrive:
> He guides me and the bird. In his good time! [1]

XII

Not To Be Feared

"Because I live, ye shall live also." John 14:19

SOMETIMES DEATH COMES SUDDENLY, UNEXPECTEDLY. AT such times we need especially to hear God speaking his message of hope and comfort to us.

None of us go very far through life before we face the experience of a loved one being taken from us. We feel, don't we, so very much alone? God in his own wisdom has created it this way. Yet we are not alone, for we share one with another in the passing of a loved one. For a moment let us think of a young prophet who also was sad and who felt very, very much alone.

King Uzziah had been called to face his God, and the young Isaiah was staggered by the blow. Uzziah, possibly with the exception of David, had done more than any other ruler to help his people. Now he was no longer with them. But suddenly, in all his sorrow and confusion, a new power and strength came to Isaiah.

In a vision he saw the Lord sitting on a throne watching him, and he realized that in and behind life was God, keeping watch over his own. He was a God who was with him and would help him, a God from whom we all come and to whom we shall go.

Now in our own day and in our own situation we ask:

but what difference does it make if he is with us? How can God help us? And there comes the answer: he can help us in many ways. Like he did to Isaiah, he can point out to our souls through the Holy Spirit that death itself is not to be feared—that there are greater tragedies in life and living than death. Through faith, therefore, we commit our loved ones, knowing all will be well.

At Easter we celebrate the Master's resurrection and his conquering of death. "Because I live, ye shall live also," said Jesus. What a comfort it is to realize that our loved one has been taken to a place which Christ has prepared for him.

Some of you have on your shelves the book *A Man Called Peter*. You will remember the scene in which Peter Marshall was being taken to the hospital. He smiled at his wife and said, "See you in the morning."

Mrs. Marshall didn't realize that they would be his final words to her.[1] Yet how full they were of Christian faith. For Peter Marshall there would be no darkness that night, but only the light of heaven and eternity.

We, too, can say to our loved ones in spirit when they are called, "See you in God's morning." At that time, spirit with spirit, we shall be united one with another.

Not only is death, then, not to be feared, but our loved one, because of what death actually is, would bid us look up and be lifted up. After all, how can we be depressed when something wonderful has hapepned to one we love? Would we wish to call him back from the glories of heaven to the things of this earth? Death is not something to be

59

morbidly feared; it is to be maturely accepted when God decides to call us.

Tennyson had such an attitude toward death. One day he realized that his time on this earth was short. He had faith in immortality and understood its wonderful message for him. As he was thinking of these things one day, there came to his mind a familiar picture.

He thought of the narrow strait separating the Isle of Wight from the shores of England. How often at eventide he had crossed it! He recalled the beautiful sunsets, the tinkling of the cowbells on the mainland, the noise of the water on the sandy bar—how peaceful the scene was and how much he enjoyed crossing the narrow strip of water. With this in mind he began to write, thinking as he did so of his call that was shortly to come through death and hoping that his loved ones would realize that it would be just as beautiful as his rowing was from the Isle of Wight to the shores of England.

> Sunset and evening star,
>   And one clear call for me!
> And may there be no moaning of the bar,
>   When I put out to sea,
>
> But such a tide as moving seems asleep,
>   Too full for sound and foam,
> When that which drew from out the boundless deep
>   Turns again home.
>
> Twilight and evening bell,
>   And after that the dark!

And may there be no sadness of farewell,
   When I embark;

For tho' from out our bourne of Time and Place
   The flood may bear me far,
I hope to see my Pilot face to face
   When I have crost the bar.[2]

XIII

The First Five Minutes

"For as in Adam all die, even so in Christ shall all be made alive."   *I Cor. 15:22*

CLARENCE MACARTNEY ONCE TOLD OF AN OFFICER HOME from India. The man had served for forty years there and had retired to spend his last days in the garden lands of England. One day friends persuaded him to give them an account of his experiences. He told them of battles, sieges, ambushes, and surprise attacks. They listened with breathless interest. At the conclusion he said, "I expect to see someday something more thrilling than anything I have yet seen." They were surprised. They said, "It is impossible!" Then he continued softly, "I expect to see it the first five minutes after death."

In the heart of that Indian officer was a strong belief in immortality—an immortality that is within reach of us all, through Jesus Christ who is our Saviour.

Each time we come in loving memory to commit a loved one unto God, we, too, would affirm our faith in immortality. For out of our faith we look upon death not as an end, but as a shadowed valley leading to a fuller life. It means simply, in fact, a transition of personality from this life to the one which has been prepared for us.

Life is full of transitions. We go through the period of babyhood, then childhood, youth, the middle years, and old age. Throughout it all, changes have taken place in the body form, but the essential *you* is still there. Science tells us that before we are forty years old we have undergone six complete changes of body. Yet the personality is carried on through them all.

Now, when death comes, he who wastes not a leaf nor a twig would scarcely waste a personality nurtured by him through these other changes of life. As his own end was approaching a few years ago, William N. Clarke wrote the following lines, which bear this out:

> Gone, they tell me is youth,
> Gone the strength of my life,
> Nothing remains but decline,
> Nothing but age and decay.
>
> Not so! I am God's little child,
> Only beginning to live.
> Coming the days of my prime,
> Coming the strength of my life,
> Coming the vision of God,
> Coming my bloom and my power! [1]

This experience of death, then, comes to us all. It cannot be side-stepped. We cannot remain forever children, nor can we remain forever adults. These physical bodies are but temporary temples for the souls within us, and we must face this. Some people are not willing to face this fact of death. A former king, Louis of France, was one of these. He ordered that no one mention the word "death" in his presence. By this method he hoped to avoid it—how foolish! Death is not something to be feared, but to be understood. Just as at birth we are released from the body which contains us, so at death we are released from this body which contains our spirit; and it becomes not death, but a birth into something higher.

Our responsibility, then, is to have a spirit—a spirit through Christ Jesus, worthy to be carried into eternity. God has given to each one of us unique power to destroy or nurture his spirit within us. Instead of fearing the end let us each build spiritually and morally a soul-personality that will be immune to death. A soul that when death comes will be acceptable in the sight of God. This will be an earnest endeavor. It will mean honest craftmanship. We might stumble here and fall there, but God will not examine too carefully our blundering workmanship as long as there are sincere and willing hands attempting to do his will. It requires faith to believe this and faith to live this out. At one point in Bunyan's *Pilgrim's Progress* we see two pilgrims, Christian and Hopeful, coming down to the river. When they behold the width and depth of the river they are stunned. Then they meet two persons whose raiment and faces shine like gold.

They ask them if there is no other way to get across to the gates of the holy city. Are there no boats, no bridges, no fords that they might use to cross?

"You must go through or you cannot enter the gate," they are told. The pilgrims have still another question to ask: "Is the water all of the same depth?"

"You shall find it deeper, or shallower, as you believe in the King of the place," is the answer they hear.

Christian begins to cry out, "I sink in deep waters." But Hopeful cries, "Be of good cheer, my brother: I feel the bottom, and it is good."

As we think of this scene, there come next the words of the Scriptures: "When thou passest through the waters, I will be with thee; and through the rivers, they shall not overflow thee." Bearing in mind these reassuring words, we know that we, too, can pass through the waters of death and find the gate of the place which he has gone to prepare for us. Our souls will have then found their permanent home, at rest and in peace with their God.

> Though earth and man were gone,
>   And suns and universes ceased to be,
> And Thou wert left alone,
>   Every existence would exist in Thee.
>
> There is not room for Death,
>   Nor atom that his might could render void:
> Thou—THOU art Being and Breath,
>   And what Thou art may never be destroyed.[2]

XIV

Only a Line

"Why seek ye the living among the dead?" Luke 24:5

LESLIE WEATHERHEAD WAS ONE NIGHT ABOARD A SHIP which was cutting through the Mediterranean Sea. The boat passed quite close to Stromboli, an island volcano rising sheer out of the sea.

When the word spread that they were passing this island, men rushed up to line the railing to watch it. It grew dark. Suddenly a great burst of flame shot up from the crater at the summit, and they could see red-hot boulders rolling down the mountainside. Gradually a tongue of red lava forced its way down to the sea. As the ship passed by, the outline of the island disappeared; but the hot stream of lava, like a great, open, glowing wound, sliced the darkness. As Weatherhead asked: What did it mean? It meant that for a few hours there had been revealed to those privileged few the great fires from the earth's heart, which have been burning since the world began.[1]

Like the fires of Stromboli on a dark night, we have seen God's everlasting love in a darkened world—revealing something of his inward nature and his holy purpose for men.

As we draw close to the purpose of God, we find in it that which can help us in our sorrow. In the hour of bereavement we momentarily join another little group who also were sorrowing.

There they were, standing near where they believed their loved one was resting. I am thinking of the garden of Joseph of Arimathea, where the two Marys and Joanna were standing outside the sepulchre. To them came two angels in white, who said, "Why seek ye the living among the dead?"

For a moment they were puzzled; then slowly the great truth penetrated their grief. There they were, confronted by the Christ himself, and the full meaning of the empty tomb burst upon them. Here was One who knew! Here was One who cared! The hymn writer Frank E. Graeff put it this way:

> Does Jesus care when I've said "good-bye"
>   To the dearest on earth to me,
> And my sad heart aches Till it nearly breaks
>   Is it aught to Him? does he see?
> O Yes, He cares, I know He cares,
>   His heart is touched with my grief;
> When the days are weary, The long nights dreary,
>   I know my Saviour cares.[2]

God does know and care about us! Throughout the Bible pages one can't help sensing this caring, this thoughtfulness of Jesus. His concern for the troubled and the helpless around him was everywhere evident. He noticed the man who was lame, the man who was blind. He even took notice of a little child whose stomach was rumbling with hunger. Page after page records how sensitive he was to not only their physical needs but also their spiritual and moral suffering. As a result, he was so able to enter into the feelings and the conditions of his people.

We are told that a distinguished naturalist was one day pushing his way through a tangled thicket in a mountain region in Jamaica. Suddenly he came upon the most magnificent orchid he had ever seen. He began to reflect on how long it had been growing unnoticed. Then he thought to himself, "To what purpose is this waste?"

A few moments later the true answer came into his soul: "Speak not of waste. Can only man admire beauty?" [3] God was aware of it. God is aware of us. As part of his family, not only is he aware of us, but he seeks to share with us the beauty and purpose of eternity. As children of immortality we come, recognizing death for what it is.

As we accept God's purpose, through Jesus, death becomes a line, nothing more, that sooner or later is drawn by God across life's pathway. It is not the end of things, but a line that shuts us out, because of our human limitations, to the glories and richness beyond. And if we are faithful servants, these things will be revealed in God's good time to each of us.

It means that with courage we can face the future. With new purpose we seek to live better, knowing that in us God's holy purpose will be fulfilled. Then, when death comes for us, it will be but a line over which we step to those we love; and we shall understand the words of the Bible, "Why seek ye the living among the dead?"

Yet Love will dream, and Faith will trust,
(Since He who knows our need is just,)
That somehow, somewhere, meet we must.
Alas for him who never sees
The stars shine through his cypress-trees!
Who, hopeless, lays his dead away,
Nor looks to see the breaking day
Across the mournful marbles play!
Who hath not learned, in hours of faith,
    The truth to flesh and sense unknown,
That Life is ever lord of Death,
    And Love can never lose its own! [4]

XV

On Being Ready

"Therefore be ye also ready: for in such an hour as ye think not the Son of man cometh."　　　*Matt. 24:44*

THESE WORDS OF MATTHEW MIGHT SEEM LIKE STRANGE words, and as we read them we might ask ourselves: "Ready for what?" It would be foolish for me to say that we should look forward to the coming of death. Anyone who is normal at all with red blood in his veins wants to live. Yet here the words of the scripture point out that, even though we might like to live and though we enjoy thoroughly our living, we should live in such a way that when God calls us the state of our souls, at a moment's notice, may be ready to enter the glories of heaven. It means that our thoughts and living, at all times, must be acceptable to God. Then at such an hour as he chooses, we will be ready. Archer Wallace, in his book *Autograph of God,* tells that four centuries ago a young soldier of Italy stood before a very devout monk, Philip Neri, and told him of his military ambition. The monk asked the youth how far he might advance. Would he ever become a captain? The boy thought it possible. "What then?" again asked the monk. The young soldier's eyes began to shine as he said, "Maybe someday I might even become a great general." The boy's daydreaming was shattered as Philip Neri, looking him

70

squarely in the eyes, spoke softly once more the words: "What then?" Then there began to dawn on the young soldier's mind what Neri meant. Even if, step by step, he advanced, at the end of it all what would he have, or what would he really be? It is possible that at this point there came into his mind the old familiar words: "For what shall it profit a man, if he shall gain the whole world, and lose his own soul?"[1]

The decisions before each one of us in life today aren't always easy to make. We are constantly faced with choices. And here, for many of us, lies the problem. We are content merely with good. It gets us by. In comparison with others it's not so bad, but it's not our best. For a follower of Jesus this will never do. It is at this point that the real cultivation of our souls must begin. We must strive, even as Jesus did, for the ultimate good we are capable of accomplishing. Then, no matter where we are in our climb when death's hand is placed upon us, the attitudes of our souls will be right, and we shall be ready.

Our text points out: "For in such an hour as ye think not" we might meet the Master. We won't pick the time, but God will! Our concern, then, is not with the quantity of life that we shall have, but with the quality of life we are living. As we consider the quality which we are going to put into life, let us realize that all of life—our birth, the air we breathe, the blessings we enjoy—come from him. He is the source. We are his people, and our actions ought to reflect his thought and purpose.

We all, at some time or other, have seen the sun set.

71

Many of you will recall happy moments spent watching the sun sink across a lake. Then when the sun had gone down and could no longer be seen itself, its light, reflected on the clouds, painted a glorious scene across the sky.

In a spiritual way our souls have been created by God to act as skies reflecting his glory and purpose.

> By looking to Jesus, Like Him thou shalt be;
> Thy friends in thy conduct His likeness shall see.[2]

Certain lives, like living sunsets, seem to bear this out. Some years ago in our church a young man was teaching a boys' class in Sunday school. He was stricken with polio and was paralyzed for many months—a helpless cripple. Though at times he became discouraged, he never gave up. He even attempted to earn his own living and had set up in his room a small printing press. His courage and faith were admired by all. The boys of his class no longer had him for a teacher, yet by his example he continued to teach them. One found that spending an afternoon with him was a most rewarding and enriching experience. Without any exaggeration one could say that in his life there was reflected part of the glory of God.

Not only when we are sick or in trouble, but at all times, let us think of these things and realize how close we are to God. Let us not be too busy to do this. Let us live strongly and kindly, striving to be the best we can. In so doing we will reveal his spirit and be ready for the hour when we shall meet our Lord face to face.

Some day the silver cord will break,
   And I no more as now shall sing;
But O, the joy when I shall wake
   Within the palace of the King!
And I shall see Him face to face,
And tell the story—Saved by Grace.[3]

XVI

My Shepherd

"The Lord is my shepherd; I shall not want." Ps. 23:1

LEGEND HAS IT THAT ONCE UPON A TIME IN PERSIA A shepherd boy became king. In his palace he kept one room for his simple shepherd things—his staff, water cruse, cloak, and food pouch. He kept that room as a reminder that he was once only a shepherd boy.

Long before Jesus came, another shepherd boy became king. The world has never been allowed to forget that he was once a shepherd, not because he kept a room with his shepherd's things in it, but because he revealed his faith and grasp of God in a power poem written in the language of his boyhood—the language of a shepherd. And as a result we have today the twenty-third Psalm.

When we come in the presence of death, how helpful are the words: "Yea, though I walk through the valley of the shadow of death, I will fear no evil: for thou art with me; thy rod and thy staff they comfort me."

Picture this boyhood scene with me, if you will. There is need for new pasture, for the fields are brown. The shepherd prepares to break camp; he gathers his sheep around him and begins the descent into the valley. Down the rocky slopes he carefully guides them, watching for lurking animals that might harm them or loose stones that might crush their feet. They cross the wind-swept, sunless

74

valley floor and finally ascend to bright rich meadows safely beyond.

Years later, when confronted by death, our shepherd king remembered this scene of his boyhood. Just as the shepherd led his sheep down into the darkness of the valley, so would the Lord, the great Shepherd of us all, lead us through the valley of death into the fields of glory.

This picture of God as Shepherd appears a little later in the scriptures, where we read in Isaiah: "He shall feed his flock like a shepherd: He shall gather the lambs with his arm, and carry them in his bosom, and shall gently lead those that are with young."

Jesus himself, coming from God, fulfilled and accepted this role of a shepherd. "I am the good shepherd, and know my sheep, and am known of mine." Surely here we see a warm, personal relationship between the Master and those he has come to lead.

How often people look upon this life as a permanent abode. It's not. If we are to follow the good Shepherd, then life becomes a pathway to something better. Where will he lead us? The answer to this age-old query can be found in the fourteenth chapter of the Gospel of John: "In my Father's house are many mansions: if it were not so, I would have told you. I go to prepare a place for you. And if I go and prepare a place for you, I will come again, and receive you unto myself; that where I am, there ye may be also."

As we are led by the good Shepherd into the light of the great mansions, we shall come not as strangers, but as loved ones, into the presence of One we already know. For here will be the God to whom we prayed when we were boys and girls. Here will be the God we worshiped in Sunday school and later in church, the God we know well and who knows us well, the God who calls us his children—a Father God who loves us even more dearly than a shepherd loves his lambs.

We all remember, don't we, the old story of the lad who was coming home late at night across the moor? The night was dark. Every new sound or dark shadow made the boy's heart leap with fear. Suddenly there appeared out of the mist before him the shadow of what seemed to be a great monster. The lad froze, paralyzed with fear. Then before his very eyes the monster turned into the familiar figure of his father who had come to meet him. No longer did the shadows of the misty moor cast over him their spell of fear, for he was not alone—his father was with him.

Along the pathways of life may the good Shepherd lead and guide us, and as each of us enters into the shadows of death when his time comes, may we find there the arms of a Father ready to receive us.

> I cannot think of them as dead
> Who walk with me no more
> Along the path of life I tread;
> They have but gone before.
>
> The Father's house is mansioned fair
> Beyond my vision dim;
> All souls are His, and here or there
> Are living unto Him.[1]

XVII

On a Gray Day

*"Whom have I in heaven but thee? . . . God is the
strength of my heart, and my portion for ever."*
Ps. 73:25-26

"WHOM HAVE I IN HEAVEN BUT THEE?" HERE WE FIND
not so much a question as a statement of fact. One Sunday
recently we received a number of children through holy
baptism into the church. From childhood up they will be
taught, as we were taught, that God is their heavenly
Father, which indicates that they must be his children.
How difficult it is to describe what it means to be a child
of God!

Now, as his children there is much of life we do not
understand. Like the psalmist of old, we do not understand
the prosperity of the wicked. We see on all sides the suffering of many good Christian people. Our papers are
filled with accounts of innocent people being hurt. Yet as
children of God we are sure of and understand certain
things, and like the psalmist we are convinced that true
and lasting peace lies in daily communion with our God.
Though all else might fail us, including these earthly
bodies, God, here and in heaven, is everlasting and eternal.

Leslie Weatherhead, one day while on his vacation, was
roaming the hills of the Scottish border near Tweedsmuir,
where John Buchan loved to walk. It was a gray day with

an occasional fall of rain; the higher he climbed, the foggier it became, and the valley seemed like a vast cauldron of mist all swirling around. Now and then a ray of sunlight would burst through, lighting up a little stream or a patch of purple heather in all its glory. Then it would fade and be all clouds again, and he thought, "Which is the abiding reality—the darkness or the light?" In the mood which he was in he was beginning to wonder.

As he climbed still higher and finally reached the summit, he came to the realization that though the fog and the mist appeared to be prevailing, they were really only temporary patches here and there. He knew that one hundred feet above him, and above everything else, was the light of the sun.[1]

How true we find this of life; like the psalmist, in our loneliness and bereavement we can raise our eyes of faith upward and behold the light and glory of God, which is for all men.

After declaring this fact about the permanence of God, the writer of our text declares that God is able to impart to our souls something of his own stability and endurance. In so doing he becomes the strength of our hearts. Not only is our God everlasting, but through our Lord and Saviour he imparts everlasting things to us.

Russel Ditzen, sitting one day in the Palmer House in Chicago, was admiring the pillars and the ceiling when a friend said, "All this will go quickly in terms of the long sweep of time. Only the things of the mind and spirit endure." As his friend spoke these words, Russel Ditzen thought he was being unduly pessimistic. After the Palmer

78

House was destroyed, Ditzen wrote, "I know my friend was right. What really abides is of the mind and of the spirit." [2] Buildings come and go, but the things of the mind and spirit go on forever.

Therefore, as Christian people we thank God for the eternal things which can be built within our souls. We thank him for the hope of eternity which is available for us all, and for the fact that he is our father and does watch over us. Better than words of mine, the following little poem gathers up our thoughts:

When the storms of life are raging,
    Tempests wild on sea and land.
I will seek a place of refuge
    In the shadow of God's hand.

Though He may send some affliction,
    'Twill but make me long for home;
For in love and not in anger,
    All His chastenings will come.

So, while here the cross I'm bearing,
    Meeting storms and billows wild,
Jesus for my soul is caring,
    Naught can harm His Father's child. [3]

XVIII

At Peace

"Peace I leave with you, my peace I give unto you."
John 14:27

WHAT THOUGHTS COME TO YOUR MIND WHEN YOU THINK of the word "peace"? Some of us might think of a quiet walk in a garden at eventide, where even the birds themselves seem quiet. Others might think of a special path, winding through the stillness of a woods. As you walk along that path, you breathe in the clean, fresh smell of the trees; and you do more than this—you breathe in also something of their quietness and serenity. As I write this, I am sitting on a cliff overlooking Lake Huron. The sun has been sinking in the west, and the only noise—the lapping of the water on the beach. Where could one find more peaceful surroundings?

It is said that Robert Louis Stevenson, on the island of Samoa, would often go out on troubled days to a nearby hill. There he would gaze at a great bank of clouds until something of the peace of the scene filled his soul.

This peace which we receive from our surroundings is good as far as it goes, but it fails to go deep enough. In the Bible we read of "the peace of God, which passeth all understanding." Here is the type of peace that Jesus spoke of. Whether the weather is stormy or fair, it is a peace that brings about a serenity of soul. It creates a state of mind that finds an adjustment to the total order of things, producing a balance of the soul and resulting in wholeness of living.

One cannot simply be at peace with the material world, for it changes so often. We might stand admiring a sunset on a seashore, but what happens to our inward being when a storm shatters the serenity of the sky? The same thing is equally true of our daily living, for suddenly the black cloud of death looms in a formerly clear sky, and our peace is gone. But if a man or woman finds a peace arising out of a true balance of soul, as he or she sincerely seeks to fulfill the will of God, he will grant to each a spirit such that, no matter whether the sky is light or dark, he will be able to face life as he meant them to. The question then on our minds is—how can we find such a peace? The answer comes—we find it as we pursue the right aims in life. Jesus' peace was based on his right relationship to his Father. The direction of his life was the direction set by his Father's will as he, in obedience, sought to fulfill it.

There is a story told about Wendell Phillips. One night he was talking to a young friend about the heroic days of the past. As the young man was leaving, he said, "Mr. Phillips, if I had lived in your time, I think I would have been heroic too."

The old man put his hands on the boy's shoulder and said, "You are living in my time and in God's time. . . . No man would have been heroic then who is not heroic now." [1]

> Mourn not for vanished ages,
>   With their great heroic men,

Who dwell in history's pages,
　　And live in the poet's pen,
For the grandest times are before us
　　And the world is yet to see,
The noblest worth of this old earth,
　　Is the men that are to be.[2]

In following today God's path of duty and service, we, too, can be heroic and out of it all will emerge his peace. But at this some of us might object. Ah, yes! How nice to think of a state of peace awaiting us in the future! But is there nothing to help us now? And the answer is, of course, "yes"; this peace is not simply a dream of the future, but reality in the present as well as in the future. Jesus did not say, "My peace I will hold for you," but he did say, "My peace I leave with you," so that in the following of his eternal purpose we can emerge from the trials and bereavements—purified, strengthened, at peace. Through the difficulties of life he will guide us until we are ready to step through the doorway of death to the greater peace beyond.

A few years ago, while stationed at Calgary during the war years, several of us in our Air Force flight decided to spend a holiday week end at Banff. We wrote to reserve rooms or a cottage. It was during the busy tourist season and rooms were hard to get. In answer to our letter we were told we could obtain a cabin about one half mile from Banff station. The proprietor even said that he would meet us at the station so that we wouldn't lose our way.

He did. It was dark when we met him. We found he was

a local guide. We walked up and along many paths into the foothills through rows of trees until finally we came to his clearing. One of the boys, when we stopped, said, "Don't you ever get lost up here?" And the guide smilingly answered, "How could I? I know the way." He threw open the door of the cabin. The light had been left on. It shone out through the open doorway inviting us to step in.

By faith, we follow One who, through life and death, not only knows the way, but said, "I am the way." Just as the door of the little cabin in that pine clearing was opened by the guide, revealing the light within to us, so does the Master seek, by his presence, to open for us the doorway to the glories of heaven. He offers to share with us a life and peace which we can carry across death's threshold into the brightness of heaven beyond.

Peace does not mean the end of all our striving,
    Joy does not mean the drying of our tears;
Peace is the power that comes to souls arriving
    Up to the light where God Himself appears.

Joy is the wine that God is ever pouring
    Into the hearts of those who strive with Him,
Light'ning their eyes to vision and adoring,
    Strength'ning their arms to warfare glad and grim.[3]

XIX

Preparing for Glory

"Even so, come, Lord Jesus." Rev. 22:20

HOW OFTEN WE HAVE VISITED FRIENDS AND LOVED ONES IN the hospital and found that though their spirits were good, their flesh was weak. They had fought the fight, they had run life's race, their course was almost completed. With sadness we left them, knowing that the next time we called they might be no longer with us. Still, back of our sadness there was a belief that what God wills is best. Our loved ones who are sick often realize this better than we. I have the feeling that they do not always share with us in our desire for them to remain with us. In their illness, as they draw near their end, they seem to sense something of the glory which awaits them. So it was with John on the island of Patmos, where he wrote the words of the scripture: "Even so, come, Lord Jesus."

A few years ago a man who had worked hard in a big city all his life retired to an acre of land in a nearby county. On his land he built a small, but comfortable house. I knew him well.

Several weeks ago when near his house I stopped, not because I saw him out, but because the windows were boarded up. The weeds were starting to grow on the path, and there were no signs of life. A farmer was passing by;

I stopped him and asked him where my friend was. He told me that he had passed away that spring after an illness of almost a year. Quickly there came into my mind the thought, as I looked at the boarded up little house: "It's too bad." Then another thought came: "Do I mean that?" No longer was he able to enjoy this life. He had been a good man. Why would we call him back?

> If God hath made this world so fair,
>   Where sin and death abound,
> How beautiful, beyond compare,
>   Will paradise be found! [1]

So it is that when our loved ones are taken after their threescore years and ten, we would not call them back, even if we could—for a greater love than ours is operating back of life.

One of the great mercies that God has provided for us is that when our physical bodies fail, it releases our souls from them and takes us unto himself. After all, God's wisdom is above and beyond the wisdom of man.

Now, not only in this great Christian text, "Even so, come, Lord Jesus," is there a desire to meet God personally, but it also reveals a joy at such a meeting—in anticipating such a meeting. Death has been overcome. The darkness of grief can also be overcome as we share in the joy of what eternity really means. We can prepare for it by the life we live and the way we live it now.

John had done his work as best he could. As a prisoner on the island of Patmos he could do little, but what he

85

could he did. He did not fear the outcome. His faith was great and his belief in the ultimate purpose of Jesus was tremendous. God's kingdom, someday, would destroy the darkness of the world; and when God called him, in particular, he would be ready.

His was a faith based on the value that he believed God placed on human lives. As we realize how much value God does put on us, his human children, there ought to be a similar faith and certainty, even in our mourning, about life and the end of life—the thing we call death. For through faith God does not let us remain in the valley of desolation.

Many of us, several years ago, heard the famous Toyohiko Kagawa when he spoke in the city of Toronto. Our hearts were thrilled with the stories he told of Christianity's growth in Japan.

On one occasion, Dr. Kagawa told of a man who came to a hospital suffering from a terrible oriental disease. At one time he had thought the only cure was to take his life and to end his suffering. However, he came to this particular hospital for treatment. They told him there was a cure, but that his body would have to be immersed in a chemical solution for a long time. He agreed and stepped into a bathtub for seven long years. Night and day he lay, not leaving it, his body completely covered with this solution; even his arms were covered.

As the days went by he grew bitter, until one day he remembered words he had heard on the market square. A missionary had spoken them. He asked for a New Testament. They brought him one. The question now was—how could he read it? They quickly solved it by hanging the Testament over the bathtub so that he could read it as he lay in the solution, and from time to time they would turn the pages.

As the Word of God was read, salvation came unto his soul. No longer was he just a man in the bathtub; he was a child of God. Through Christ and his Cross the diseased man realized the value that God placed upon him. It lifted him up, and his despair was replaced with a certainty of faith that God had a purpose for him.

God places a value upon us all. For each and every living child he has a purpose to be fulfilled. Let us work at it like John, with certainty and joy; and when we enter into the twilight of our life, then we, too, can say, as he did: "Even so, come, Lord Jesus."

> God did anoint thee with his odorous oil,
> To wrestle, not to reign; and he assigns
> All thy tears over, like pure crystallines,
> For younger fellow-workers of the soil
> To wear for amulets. So others shall
> Take patience, labor, to their heart and hand,
> From thy hand and thy heart and thy brave cheer,
> And God's grace fructify through thee to all.
> The least flower, with a brimming cup, may stand
> And share its dewdrop with another near.[2]

XX

The Great Divide

"O Lord, by these things men live." Isa. 38:16

SOME OF US HAVE VISITED THAT PLACE IN WESTERN
Canada known as the Great Divide. Signs mark the spot.
On one side of the ridge the water runs to the Pacific
Ocean, and on the other it makes its way across the flat
prairies and eventually finds its outlets in the Hudson Bay.

There are different kinds of divides in life; and as we
stand in the presence of death, we, of course, come to the
great divide of all. Though death constantly comes between
us and our loved ones, yet we believe that through faith it
is but a separation between the life we live on earth and
the life Jesus promised we shall live in heaven.

The resurrection of the Master has changed the picture
of death for us. We can't see over the ridge with human
eyes, still we do realize that it can be crossed. When death
comes to those who love God, it will be in the presence of
Christ that they shall make their crossing into that realm
which is run according to the plan of heaven. Death, then,
is really not death in the sense we understand it to be, but
a continuation of life. We turn to life then. What is it?
How should we live it?

Our text states that there are certain things in life that
help us to live it and by which all men should gauge their

living. "O Lord, by these things men live." These were the words of a king, Hezekiah, who himself came very close to death in a time not unlike our own. There were wars and rumors of wars. Fear, then as today, cut its paralyzing swath across men's lives. Sin bit deeply, robbing life of its richness and best. Yet, in spite of all, he came to certain conclusions about life, and so must we. Among them is the knowledge that none of us can live without God.

Basking in the luxury of his palace, surrounded by the things of life he had collected, Hezekiah, when threatened by death, realized that these things of earth had no real claim upon him—no real sustaining value. But in it all he still had a God he could cling to, and this he did, knowing that his God had not left him.

Some months ago Ralph W. Sockman told the Chicago Sunday Evening Club of how a lawyer had as a child experienced this closeness of God to himself.

My religious faith can be expressed in a boyhood experience. I was taken by my father to New York City. I was little, and to keep from getting lost I clung to his finger, but after a while, in the crowds and the long steps, I grew tired, and my fingers began to slip, and I looked up to him and said, "Father, you'll have to take hold of my hand now. I can't hold on much longer." [1]

And we can all imagine, can't we, how his father's hand grasped the little hand of his son and helped him through the crowds? How true of life! Without the knowledge of

God's presence with us and his hand holding ours, we just couldn't face these experiences that come upon us.

"Come unto me, all ye that labour and are heavy laden, and I will give you rest," said Jesus. We take him at his word! We come to him, and in him we find life!

No! We cannot live without God! Neither can we live without the forgiveness of our God! Into the darkest recesses of our souls this forgiveness comes to clear away the obstacles that so often prevent the cleansing, revealing light of Christ. As the obstacles are cleared away, his light enters and drives back the darkness, revealing that a new and holy start can be ours.

Charlotte Elliott put it beautifully:

> Just as I am! Thou wilt receive,
> Wilt welcome, pardon, cleanse, relieve;
> Because Thy promise I believe,
> O Lamb of God, I come.[2]

These aren't simply pleasing lines. They are words of living truth! For from the Lamb of God there comes a spirit that develops within us a new and holy purpose for living.

English scientists recently disclosed that everywhere in that little island, deep within the soil, are literally hundreds of thousands of tropical plant seeds. Lying dormant for centuries, they await a change that will bring the moist warmth of the tropics, and then they will immediately spring forth in rich, green foilage.

In the realm of everyday living we need not wait for changing climates. Through God's forgiving and redeeming grace, holy and immortal things can be cultivated within

90

us. It is our duty and our Christian privilege to see that they grow!

If we cannot live without God and his forgiveness through Christ Jesus, surely we cannot live without sharing that presence and that forgiveness with others. Is there any better way of cultivating our own souls than simply revealing him to others?

The other night I had the occasion to visit a hospital in a nearby town. I had never been to that hospital before. It was dark, and I didn't know where it was. Stopping by a group of boys standing near their bicycles, I asked, "Could anyone tell me where the hospital is?" One boy straightened up quickly and answered with a smile, "I'll do better than that, sir; I'll show you where it is!" With a leap he was on his bicycle, and I followed him as he showed me the way.

How we all need, at times, to be shown the way! How we all, at times, can show the way! Out of the darkness of despair, of grief, of discouragement and loneliness, Jesus leads us. We can share him as we, too, go out into life, resolved to lead others, with God's help, until they find the grasp of the Father's hand upon them—until they find life and where it leads; then they, too, will believe that there are things by which men can die, by which men shall live.

> Thank God! there is always a Land of Beyond
>   For us who are true to the trail;
> A vision to seek, a beckoning peak,

A farness that never will fail;
A pride in our soul that mocks at a goal,
A manhood that irks at a bond,
And try as we will, unattainable still,
Behold it, our Land of Beyond! [3]

XXI

Full of the Right Things

*"I will lift up mine eyes unto the hills, from whence
cometh my help."*   Ps. 121:1

WHEN THE PSALMIST OF OLD CAME UPON AN EXPERIENCE
of life which was beyond his understanding or which
distressed him, he would raise his eyes unto the hills. In so
doing he would see them as symbols of God's everlasting
mercy and presence. "I will lift up mine eyes unto the
hills, from whence cometh my help."

In our bereavements we, too, are conscious of the hills
of God and his abiding presence. Because we are all different and are of different ages, death can appear to us
in different ways.

When it takes a child from a parent or cuts off a young
person in the prime of life, it appears tragic to us. But an
altogether different picture is presented when a loved one,
after the completion of a long life, is taken into the higher
service. Yet, no matter when it comes or how it appears to
us, there is always sadness at the parting. When it is
present with us, we, too, can raise our eyes and become
aware of the fact that just as God was with the Psalmist,
he also is with us.

Some of our loved ones live a long life, more than the
usual span of years; and as we think of those long, well-

spent years, the thought comes: "What are we putting into our years? Are we filling life with the right things?"

Now we, ourselves, cannot determine the number of our days or the years which we shall live, yet all of us can determine what we do with our days and what we do with the years we are granted. This was brought home once very forcibly to me.

On the outskirts of the city of Toronto there was, some years ago, a little mission church. The congregation wasn't strong enough in numbers to have a full-time minister, and I used to preach there as a student on the week ends. About one block from the church there lived an old man, well up in his eighties. He used to plant and care for a little flower garden which surrounded the church. Many were the beautiful flowers that grew there, and lovingly were they looked after. I asked him one day why he spent so much time fixing up the flower beds, after all, he wasn't being paid to do it.

He said, "I must keep my life full of the right things!" I wondered for awhile after that just what he meant. I know now! As long as God gave him health and years, he would use them for others in the little extra things which he did. He had found the secret of holy living, for he was actually creating within his soul an immortal attitude that would go beyond the shadow of death.

As we, too, fill our lives with the right things, they have the effect of fashioning within us, through the spirit of Jesus, qualities of the soul that will never perish.

We are told, and most of us are familiar with the story, that once upon a time in the city of Florence there was a massive block of marble. One sculptor after another had tried to make a statue of it without success. They cut and they carved it, but got nowhere. Then Michelangelo took a turn. He began by having a house built right over the block of marble. Shutting himself inside for months, he worked on the block without interruption. Finally, when he was through, the house was removed, and there stood the magnificent statue of David—now one of the glories of the world.

Under the spirit of Christ, the Master Sculptor, if we fill the years God gives to us with holy and righteous acts, we, too, will be creating immortal things that will add to the glory of the Father. We thank God, therefore, for the hills unto which we can raise our eyes; and we pray that something of their grandeur and the presence of the One they symbolize might be found in our own life and living.

> Maker of mountains—
> Creator of their beauty and their might,
> I lift my small and human heart to Thee,
> Fill it, I pray, with something of their might,
> Their steadfastness, their high serenity;
> Sweep it with canyon winds, and wash it clean
> With clear cold water from the eternal snow,
> Let these bright torrents purge it, let all mean
> Desires and passions leave it—let me go
> Back to the lowlands, back to the crowded days,
> Poised and sustained, and ready for my part,
> Let me go back, schooled in the mountain ways,
> Bearing their old vast secrets in my heart.[1]

XXII

The Path

"Thou wilt show me the path of life: in thy presence is fulness of joy; at thy right hand there are pleasures for evermore."   Ps. 16:11

HOW THANKFUL WE ARE FOR THE WORD OF GOD WHICH reveals that the path of death is actually, and can be, a path to life and that this path to eternity begins now!

Maybe into our minds there comes the question: "But how can this be?" And the answer comes: "by faith in Jesus Christ our Lord." Many years ago, at the coming of the baby Jesus to Bethlehem, God revealed that he was not yet through with our world. He loved his people. He sought his people. Through the Master he would reveal himself, that men might find through faith a path for their feet. In finding this path—his path—they would be able to bridge the chasm that looms for each of us—the chasm of death.

When I was a small boy I spent a number of summers on my uncle's farm. One hot summer day I was playing near my uncle, who was shocking grain in a back field. He called to me and asked me to go to the house for a pail of drinking water. He suggested that if I cut through the thicket I would find it shorter. I thought this a fine idea and, on climbing the rail fence, disappeared into the brush.

The farther I went, the darker it became. It got quite frightening! Then I came upon a path, and as I made my way along it, the thought came: "What if it doesn't lead to the house?" My fears increased. Then they passed, for the trees began to thin out, and I could see fields, the top of the barn, and the house in the distance. The path did lead somewhere!

How true of life! Life's path, too, can lead somewhere—to eternity. We could mention many in the Bible whose lives bear this out. There was Enoch, who walked with God, and when his end came God simply took him. There was Elijah, who, in spite of his shortcomings, was taken up by God before the very eyes of Elisha. Above all, we could think of Jesus, who began his life in a manger, and who ended it on a cross. Yet back he came to reveal that man's pathway to death leads somewhere, and to something great. "If it were not so I would have told you," he said. We believe, through faith, that he was right.

This path will lead us, then, out of the dark shadows and the tall trees of despair until we, too, shall see the eternal home and loved ones who have gone before us.

As we make our way along this path of faith, one further thought comes to us. This path leads us into the presence of God. That is its end. Having trusted God, we'll find our faith fulfilled; for God will be there, and we shall enter into the fullness of his joy. In his presence we'll find no sin nor sorrow, but we shall find an understanding of the meaning of this life. Many of the things that puzzle us we will comprehend, and there will be peace and happiness.

H. V. Larcombe tells us that one day an eminent doctor

was seated in his study when he noticed his small son come sidling into the room and stand by his side. The doctor, preoccupied with his work, took out a coin and offered it to the boy. It was refused.

"I don't want any money, Daddy," the child replied. Surprised but still engrossed, the father opened a drawer, took out a bag of candy, and offered it to him. Again the child shook his head: "I don't want any candy, Daddy," he said. At this the doctor put down his pen, and swinging around so he could look squarely at his little son, he said: "You don't want money—nor candy—what do you want?"

"I don't want anything, Daddy; I only want to be with you," said the little fellow wistfully.[1]

As we commit our loved ones forever into the presence of their heavenly Father, may our lives, too, be worthy, that we may find the path that leads to home.

> He is a path, if any be misled;
>   He is a robe, if any naked be;
> If any chance to hunger, he is bread;
>   If any be a bondman, he is free;
>   If any be but weak, how strong is he!
> To dead men life he is, to sick men, health;
> To blind men, sight, and to the needy, wealth;
> A pleasure without loss, a treasure without stealth.[2]

XXIII

Completing Unfinished Plans

"And, lo, I am with you alway." Matt. 28:20

We come today in loving memory of a mother who has been called from our midst. Words seem so inadequate to express our thoughts. We know, in the eyes of God, the high place which mothers hold. For did not Jesus himself come to us by an earthly mother? Our hearts are sad. It is natural. Even our Lord, in an hour of sadness, wept with Mary and Martha. Yet, in our sorrow, he is here to help us and to offer us comfort. Jesus said, "I am with you always." We know how it helps when neighbors rally to share our grief. How much more does it help us when God himself shares with us the sorrow we endure. He knows our feelings—our shattered thoughts.

In Sandringham Church, Yorkshire, England, there is one of the most remarkable windows in the world. It was made of broken pieces of glass which were thrown aside as worthless rubbish. Love, care, and a lot of patience put them together again; and when the sun shines through, one can see portrayed there the figure of Christ.[1] In the spirit of Christ Jesus and by his power, we, too, can gather together our shattered thoughts and face the future for what it holds.

Not only is he with us, but he will direct us. One of the most familiar scenes in our Bible is that of the disciples

in difficulty on the Sea of Galilee. So often, when we think
of this scene, we dwell on the disciples' lack of faith; and
it is true—they did lack faith. Jesus mentioned it, but even
in their lack of faith they turned to him for direction. He
helped them. They reached the other shore. In our re-
sponsibilities to be fulfilled, he will sustain and direct us.

When we have exhausted our store of endurance,
　　When our strength has failed ere the day is half done,
When we reach the end of our hoarded resources,
　　Our Father's full giving is only begun.

His love has no limit, his grace has no measure,
　　His power no boundary known unto men;
For out of his infinite riches in Jesus
　　He giveth and giveth and giveth again.*

At this time it is good to realize that not only does he
comfort us and direct us, but that he has bestowed upon us
certain blessings.

We think first of the blessing of past dreams shared.
Neither death nor time can erase the precious things that
have been planned one with another. In our minds and in
our lives many of these things can still be carried out.

A few days ago a little girl came to my door. She sold
me a tiny red poppy. As we beheld that little red poppy,
we knew it had a story to tell. It was a story of men whose
lives were suddenly cut off before all their plans of a better
world could be completed. It told us we were the ones

---

* Annie Johnson Flint, "He Giveth More," Copyright. Reproduced
by permission. Evangelical Publishers, Toronto, Canada.

to take the torch and hold it high. How true of all of life. We, here, have been spared—for a time, at least. We have strength and ability. Let us take the things that have been planned and make them real.

Then there is the blessing of our faith and the promises it holds out to us. I recall visiting, shortly after I was ordained, an elderly man and his wife. On the piano was a picture of four grown youngsters. I asked them where they were. The mother told me where one was and then she said, "A year ago before you came, the other three lost their lives one night in an accident." I didn't know what to say! My face must have shown it. She looked at me and said softly, "Don't look so sad. There's hope in a future life, isn't there? Haven't we the faith and the hope to believe they are in the love and care of God?" How right she was! It is good to realize that our loved one is not here, but in the care of a loving God.

Yes, she'll be missed. Terrific problems will have to be faced and met. By the power of God these things, however, can be solved. With this in mind let us go now to the task before us, thankful for the hope, through Jesus, that is in us all, thankful for a presence that will comfort and direct us and enable us to fulfill the daily duties, as our loved one, if she were here, would have us do.

> God calls our loved ones, but we lose
>   not wholly
>   What He hath given;
> They live on earth, in thought and
>   deed, as truly
>   As in his heaven.[2]

XXIV

Behold the Stars

*"I the Lord have called thee . . . and will hold thine
hand, and will keep thee."*   Isa. 42:6

A FAMOUS LONDON DOCTOR TOLD A FRIEND OF HIS ONCE
that while he was reading the evening paper his two children came running in with a new discovery!

"Daddy, until the streets were darkened we never saw
the stars!" [1]

Those children didn't realize that the stars were always
shining in the sky and that it is only when the sun goes
down that we can see them!

How often we find this true of life! With the glare, the
glitter, and the noise of modern living, God's stars, for
many of us, are seldom seen. Yet, in an hour of sadness
such as this, we become aware, often for the first time, that
they are there. What are these stars?

Let us realize first, as Christian people, that we can behold the star of hope. What a difference between a person
with hope and one without hope! Our Bible tells us: "I
the Lord have called thee." We are children of a hope
that can be fulfilled as we follow out the plan God has
called us to do. Big or small, it matters not, so long as in
our soul there is the obedience to it. This hope of God
is not there because we deserve it, but because in his
102

creation he has placed the capacity in us to rise and share with him, through his Son, the spiritual re-creation of an immortal world!

In spite of dark skies, we shall find happiness and peace within our souls; and then when death comes, be it sudden or gradual, it will mean a greater sharing with God in the fellowship beyond.

Let us also behold the star of comfort—"and will hold thine hand." As we behold this second star, we are aware that immortality changes the meaning of death for us and for our loved ones. Not only are there two worlds, this one and the world to come, but through both God will accompany us. He will actually lead us—our sorrow and burden—and the weight of life's grief will be no more than we can bear!

In central Manitoba there lived, all by himself, an old man. He couldn't come to church. His legs were none too good, and the steps of the church were too much for him. He apologized one day to his minister for not coming out to hear him.

His minister reassured him that it didn't matter; God understood and was right there at all times with him.

The old man said, "Indeed I know he is." He paused. "My two boys were killed in the war. My wife is gone, and I'm all alone." Then he smiled. "But I'm not really alone." He had found the star of comfort—a comfort that comes from knowing that the Master of men is with us.

Almost rebelliously, within our souls we ask, "But why is He with us?" And through faith we behold another star, the star of reassurance. He's with us to sustain us. Yes, we

103

still suffer—God never promised that we wouldn't, but he did promise that his grace would be sufficient to enable us to face what we have to suffer. And some day, in his own good time, we'll understand the reason behind these things that confront us.

A man once asked James Whistler, the artist, if he would help him hang an exceptionally beautiful painting. "I've tried and I've failed," he said. "Perhaps you can do it!"

Whistler looked at its beauty for a moment, and he said, "Man, you can't fit that picture to the room; you must fit the room to the picture!" [2] We can't change many of the things that come to us in life, yet we can change our attitudes to fit the circumstances made by these things that come upon us so that we see them in their true light. The picture that Jesus brought of death ought to change completely the darkness in our souls; it ought to rearrange the room of our living so that there we might see glowing, even in our mourning, the star of hope, the star of comfort, the star of reassurance; for, after all, has he not called us! does he not hold us?—and will he not keep us?

> Slowly by God's hand unfurled,
> Down around the weary world
> Falls the darkness; oh, how still
> Is the working of Thy will!
> Mighty Maker! Here am I,—
> Work in me as silently,
> Veil the day's distracting sights,
> Show me heaven's eternal lights. [3]

XXV

Listening for His Footstep

"Death is swallowed up in victory." I Cor. 15:54

ON THE SIDE OF A ROAD BY THE JERICHO GATE THERE SAT
one day a number of beggars. They would shake their
begging cups and cry out for coins to those who passed
them by.

On this particular morning one beggar was not rattling
his cup like the others. He was listening intently for a
footstep—for a voice with the accent of Galilee upon it.
Then, in all that noisy street, he heard it. Taking a deep
breath, he cried with all the strength that was within him:
"Jesus, thou son of David, have mercy on me!" Jesus answered: "What wilt thou that I should do unto thee?" And
the beggar cried: "Lord, that I might receive my sight."
And Christ gave to him his sight, and he was made whole.

In a time of sorrow we commit our loved ones unto the
care of God, and like Bartimaeus of old, in a spiritual way
we would pray for sight and understanding—especially of
the meaning of death. At this point there may come to us
the following words of scripture, revealing light and giving
to us understanding which can comfort us.

"Death is swallowed up in victory." Paul knew that we
all can have victory through faith. These are confident
words. These are happy words, because they are speaking

truths that take despair from our hearts and give us hope. You will notice that it does not say death will be exchanged for victory, but rather that the element of death is swallowed up, or absorbed, in forming victory.

Here, through the hands of God, the things of sorrow, of the flesh, of this life with all its limitations, are taken and transformed into happiness, life, and fellowship above. Death, then, for those of faith, is but part of a process that loses itself in something bigger, in the presence of God.

In Byron's poem "Prisoner of Chillon," there is the story of a man who was "shut up in a dark dungeon on the shore of Lake Geneva. High up on the wall was a tiny window looking out across the lake to the mountains. The prisoner made footholds in the wall, and every day he climbed up so that he could for a moment or two look out from his prison toward the snow-clad Alps." His body was shut up within the "narrow cell but his soul was free to range the far distances." [1]

We, too, are urged to climb and to see beyond these earthly limitations. Through Jesus' healing touch, we obtain our sight and can perceive that back of the darkness of death there is hope of life, and that our loved ones, in the presence of God, will be at peace.

There is, however, another effect, not always realized. Not only is there victory over death and the knowledge that our loved ones will dwell in heaven, but also they will continue to live in memory here—now.

Are we not then each charged by God to contribute to the total output of good in our world? Nothing done in the name of God and his goodness is ever destroyed; but often unknown, its impact is felt, caught up, and reflected on down through the generations to come—over which death itself can have no effect.

Many of us, as children, have stood on a bridge and dropped stones into the quiet waters of the river below. We watched, fascinated by the ever-enlarging circle of ripples. Each circle had an effect upon the other until the outer circle touched the bank, far removed from where the stone was dropped.

Wordsworth very beautifully puts it:

> And, when the stream
> Which overflowed the soul was passed away,
> A consciousness remained that it had left,
> Deposited upon the silent shore
> Of memory, images and precious thoughts,
> That shall not die, and cannot be destroyed.[2]

So many of us today owe what we are to the ripples of love and interest that have touched our lives through the faith of those dear to us. As we think of their devotion and service, their impact is not lost upon us. Death may claim their bodies, but the spirit of what they were and the things for which they stood remain forever with us.

No wonder Paul was confident when he cried out the words of our text: "Death is swallowed up in victory." How much we, too, have to be thankful for! Let us then with confidence begin life again, realizing that there is a victory over death, that our efforts live, and that by his spirit we are used to make an impact on others.

May every soul that touches mine—
Be it the slightest contact—
Get therefrom some good;
Some little grace; one kindly thought;
One aspiration yet unfelt;
One bit of courage
For the darkening sky;
One gleam of faith
To brave the thickening ills of life,
One glimpse of brighter skies
Beyond the gathering mist—
To make this life worth while
And heaven a surer heritage.[3]

XXVI

Drawing Back the Curtain

"And underneath are the everlasting arms." Deut. 33:27

A YOUNG, NEWLY ORDAINED MINISTER HAD THE OCCASION one day to go down a prairie road. Spring had come, and although there had been only a few weeks of warm sunshine, he saw on the roadside, all by itself, a beautiful wild rose in full bloom. He stopped in amazement, and the rose seemed to say to him as he cupped it in his hand, "I am but the forerunner of thousands of wild roses which in a few short days will cover these prairies."

As the weeks passed he found this to be true—that one little rose had given him a peek into a world of beauty, the like of which he had never expected. It seemed to multiply, and in the days that followed he found that wild roses lined the roads of his parish for miles.

How often we wish that God had revealed more about heaven to us! Yet, did he not in the Master's words, like the little rose, draw back the curtain enough that we might catch a glimpse of the glory which is to come?

He told us there would be many mansions. It would be a place of holy light. Love would abound and his peace would be in us. There would be happiness, and in it all we would be reunited with those we love. What more could we want? What a wonderful picture he has portrayed here of the life that is to come! If only we will, through his words, look upward, like the young minister viewing the rose, we shall behold in part, at least, a glory that awaits us.

No matter how great our grief and sorrow, God always leaves open one great window—it is the window upward. Through it we recognize that he is near and we're not alone. Now sometimes, I know, deep down in our souls we may still cry, "God is near, but why is he near?—can he help us?" And the answer comes back swift and sure: "Yes! He is near because he is able and can help us!" And the words of the scripture, "and underneath are the everlasting arms," take on new meaning, for we can feel the grip of those arms upon us.

We human people can do certain things, can't we, at a time like this? We can come and offer our sympathy. Each of us can be a friend. Yet in it all we feel so helpless, don't we? But God, who in his Son has experienced our feeling, is able to enter into our inward being and there offer to us his balm and his peace. He made us. To him we can go. He understands us. As we look up through faith, we can receive him; and in his strength we face the todays and the tomorrows of life.

> One little hour of watching with the Master,
>   Eternal years to walk with Him in white;
> One little hour to bravely meet disaster,
>   Eternal years to reign with Him in light;
> One little hour for weary toils and trials;
>   Eternal years for calm and peaceful rest;
> One little hour for patient self-denials;
>   Eternal years for life, where life is blest.[1]

A few years ago a minister was preaching on the Glasgow green. When he was through, an opportunity was given for the public to ask questions. One man, enjoying the attention he was getting, said, "I can't see sin, or judgment, or God; therefore there can't be such things." And he continued to ridicule all that the old minister had said. When he was through, another man asked to speak. Everyone listened as he began. "Some of you may think that you are standing on grass—I can't see grass, therefore there isn't any. Some of you think that the river Clyde is near—I can't see the Clyde, therefore it can't be near. Some of you think that there is a great crowd here—I can't see a crowd, therefore there isn't one." The people looked at one another. They were standing on grass. They could see the Clyde. There was a great crowd. Then the man continued, "You are wondering why I have been talking foolishly. You see, I am blind—that's the reason I cannot see; but how foolish of me, because I can't see things, to say that they aren't there. The man before me said he couldn't see God—therefore there was no God. How foolish of him, for he too is blind—spiritually blind!" As the blind man sat down, the people caught his point and cheered him.

Through eyes of faith we do look up and see the arms of a God who not only is real but also is willing to encompass us, his children. "I will come to you. I will not leave you comfortless," said the Lord. As we think of the life of Jesus, we realize he brought comfort to all within his reach, the sick and the sin-sick, the young and the old, the weary and the down-trodden—all became recipients of

111

his love and mercy. Jesus said: "He that hath seen me hath seen the Father"—revealing once and for all that God was not only able but willing to bring help to the needy souls of his children.

We are told that Coventry Patmore did his best to rear his motherless son. One night the child, because of disobedience, was sternly rebuked and put to bed. A few hours later Coventry went up to his own bedroom and found his dressing gown pockets stuffed with the boy's toys. It was his little son's way of asking forgiveness. Going over to the lad's room, he gently placed his arms around the little fellow and kissed him.

No matter how deep our grief, let us be conscious of a heavenly Father who loves us with a greater love than that of earth, who is able and willing to lift us up to face life and what it holds for us, now and in the future.

> My house has windows that are wide and high;
>   I never keep the curtains drawn
> Lest I should miss some glory of the sky,
>   Some splendour of the breaking dawn.
>
> My soul has windows where God's sun streams in;
>   They never, never shuttered are,
> Lest their closed blinds hide in my soul some sin
>   And keep some lovely thing afar.[2]

XXVII

The Master's Garden

"Blessed are they that mourn: for they shall be comforted."   Matt. 5:4

LITTLE ONES ARE DEAR TO GOD—THIS WE KNOW. JESUS loved them and told them stories. How they must have loved him, too! What a help it is to us to realize this when God calls them back from us unto himself.

A little girl has been taken from our midst. As we mourn let us realize the ties that bind us together as friends, neighbors, and loved ones; for we, too, all love little children. We are not suffering alone, but together, upheld by the sympathy of one to another. We feel this deeply as we commit her unto the loving care of God.

Jesus said: "Blessed are they that mourn." It is natural for us to feel this way when human ties are broken. God approves, for it fulfills a very real function. It reveals our frailty—the poorness of our resources—our dependence on and closeness to God. But we are not left simply to mourn. The Bible tells us there is comfort for those who mourn.

Comfort is simply made up of two words meaning "with strength," and as we draw nigh to God in sorrow, with strength does he lift us up on new wings of faith and hope. He grants unto us an insight into what death really is so that we can come today and, in spite of our heavy hearts, realize that our little girl is not forever gone from us, but rather, she has been taken to a higher home, where compassionate arms will hold her and care for her until, in God's good time, we shall be joined again with her.

Therefore, in the spirit of our God who has made this possible and in the spirit of little children everywhere, let us turn our thoughts for a moment to a story of another little girl who was very sad, for she had just heard that she might never walk again. It's the story Ralph Connor so beautifully tells us in *The Sky Pilot*. The missionary-preacher was trying to explain how sometimes these tragic things take place, and as the child listened he began his story:

For many centuries there were only broad flat prairies across our land. One day when the Master was walking over the brown grass, he said to the prairie: "Where are your flowers, oh prairie?" And the prairie answered: "Master, I have no flower seeds."

The Master then spoke to the little birds, and they flew far and wide scattering the tiny flower seeds. After a time, again the Master walked out over his prairie, and he saw the prairies were blooming with crocuses, roses, buffalo beans, and yellow crowfoot; and though he was pleased he spoke to the prairies, "These flowers are lovely, but some are missing. Where are the clematis, columbines, violets and ferns?"

The prairie answered, "Oh Master, I cannot keep those particular flowers—the wind blows so strong and the sun
114

beats down upon my breast, and they are blown away or withered up."

Then the Master spoke to the lightning, rain, and hurricane, and they swept over the broad bosom of the prairie and washed out deep valleys and canyons; and then the little birds again planted their seeds. This time they grew, and there in the valleys that God had created were the flowers the Master loved best of all.

Then the missionary spoke to the little girl and told her that there were certain flowers which bloom only in the deep cuts of life—spiritual flowers like gentleness, meakness, long-suffering—flowers we all must grow.[1]

Surely I would be right in saying that we, too, can be happy in the knowledge that our little one has been taken to a wondrous garden around the throne of God himself. Though our hearts are very sad, because we are all going to miss her, yet let us realize, as we pass through this valley —a valley which the Master has created—that there are certain things which we can do.

Some of us will leave today and live as we have lived before—in carelessness and in indifference to the claims of God. But we all, if we will, can plant in our hearts things that will be well-pleasing to our Master, and that will be in keeping with the spirit of our little girl. Virtues she had—she who knew no evil—of gentleness, tolerance, kindness, and love—virtues which this old world needs so badly.

Let us therefore, with the help of Almighty God, plant them deep within us, that they might rise in loving memorial to a sweet little girl who was called of God.

Gracious Saviour, gentle Shepherd,
    Little ones are dear to Thee;
Gathered with Thine arms and carried
    In Thy bosom, may they be
Sweetly, fondly, safely tended,
    From all want and danger free.[2]

XXVIII

Rungs Unto Heaven

*"And behold a ladder set up on the earth, and the top of
it reached to heaven."*   Gen. 28:12

HE HAD BEEN TRAVELING. WEARY AND TIRED, HE SAW THAT
the sun was about to sink. Looking around, Jacob selected
a likely spot and pitched his little camp for the night.
Gathering together a few stones, he covered them with a
blanket, and under the twinkling stars he fell asleep. And
lo, he had a dream—a most unusual dream. "Behold a
ladder set up on the earth, and the top of it reached to
heaven." Angels of the Lord were ascending and descending, and at the top of the ladder was God himself.

The first great truth that emerges is that heaven and
earth are connected. Jacob's father had believed this, and
now for Jacob it was proving a startling thought. He saw
that the first rung of the ladder was reachable; unlike a
fire escape where you usually only can come down, this
ladder was within reach of climbing feet.

How often Jesus revealed this to be true. He taught that
hour by hour, day by day, our lives ought to be climbing
upward, drawing closer and closer to eternity. Through
faith, through our actions, and through our thoughts, this
can be done. Here in this passage, the truth is revealed
that our lives, therefore, are not lived out separate from

117

the mind that created us; but rather under the gaze of a watchful God, we are encouraged by his spirit, minute by minute, to climb upward.

Jacob saw angels ascending and descending the ladder. In other words, he was not alone. He would have an escort. Life was no lonely venture into outer space, as some people seem to think. Here in a concrete, factual way, God is showing that he would help us face life's climb —guarding and guiding us.

Sometimes we find some folk to be the type of people who dare not climb ladders for fear of growing dizzy. We found this true also during the war, in the training of pilots for the Air Force. Some student pilots were fine as long as they were looking up, but they grew fearful upon looking down. They became afraid of falling and had to be grounded. But this need not apply in the climb of life, for "the eternal God is thy refuge, and underneath are the everlasting arms"—enabling us to face the difficult bereavements, sustaining us in our climb toward him.

> 'Tis sorrow builds the shining ladder up,
> Whose golden rounds are our calamities,
> Whereon our firm feet planting, nearer God
> The spirit climbs, and hath its eyes unsealed.[1]

Not only are we never alone, then, but the ladder of life goes somewhere; it reaches heaven! The final rung is in eternity. Jesus said: "I go to prepare a place for you . . . that where I am, there you may be also." The Master didn't waste words. He knew whereof he spoke. As we realize

118

this, we see life in new perspective, for it takes on new meaning. Its end is not simply found in this world.

In the pretty little village Bourton-on-the-Water in the Cotswolds, I am told, there is a park where the town is reproduced in miniature. People can see the tiny buildings in clearest detail. It looks so real, until some bird swoops down and perches on a tiny roof. Then the model city is seen for what it is. In the hour of death we realize that life, at its very best, is short, and through Christ Jesus we see it in the perspective of eternity.

How thankful we are to God that the end of life's ladder is with him. Through faith, then, let us climb, knowing that he is with us and will lift us unto himself.

> Heaven is not reached at a single bound;
>   But we build the ladder by which we rise
>   From the lowly earth to the vaulted skies,
> And we mount to its summit round by round.
>
> I count this thing to be grandly true,
>   That a noble deed is a step toward God,
>   Lifting the soul from the common sod
> To a purer air and a broader view.
>
> We rise by the things that are under our feet;
>   By what we have mastered of good and gain,
>   By the pride deposed and the passion slain,
> And the vanquished ills that we hourly meet.[2]

119

NOTES

I. Piercing Death's Darkness

1. G. B. F. Hallock and M. K. W. Heicher, eds., *The Ministers Manual,* 1952 (New York: Harper and Brothers), p. 146.

2. Isabel Cameron, *Stories of the Doctor* (London: The Religious Tract Society, 1936), p. 18.

3. Marianne Farningham (Mary Anne Hearne), "The Father's House," Charles L. Wallis, ed., *The Funeral Encyclopedia* (New York: Harper and Brothers, 1953), pp. 228-29.

II. Brightening the Corner

1. Emily H. Miller, "Jesus Bids Us Shine."

2. Quoted in Ida Q. Moulton in A. Gordon Nasby, ed., *Treasury of the Christian World* (New York: Harper and Brothers, 1953), p. 374.

3. Ina D. Ogden, "Brighten the Corner," Copyright 1913, Renewal, 1941. The Rodeheaver Co., Owner. All Rights Reserved.

4. Quoted in J. Trevor Davies in A. Gordon Nasby, *op. cit.,* p. 37.

5. Mary Cromwell Low.

III. Returning Goodness

1. Thomas Curtis Clark, from *The Christian Century.* Used by permission of the publisher and Mrs. Thomas Curtis Clark.

2. G. A. Studdert-Kennedy, "Patience," *The Unutterable Beauty* (London: Hodder and Stoughton, Limited, 1927), p. 12.

IV. Fear Not

1. Reginald Heber, "Providence," Burton E. Stevenson, comp., *The Home Book of Verse* (New York: Henry Holt and Company, 1922), p. 3480.

2. J. W. Hart, *The Ministers Manual,* 1951, p. 121.

3. Robert Freeman, "Prayer," Virginia Ely, ed., *I Quote* (New York: George W. Stewart, Publisher, 1947), p. 291.

V. The Rock

1. Quoted in William L. Stidger, *There Are Sermons in Stories* (New York and Nashville: Abingdon Press, 1942), pp. 239-40.

2. Washington Gladden, "O Master, Let Me Walk with Thee."

3. Edward Mote, "The Solid Rock."

VI. Always Moving
1. George P. Eckman, *Studies in the Gospel of John* (Cincinnati: Jennings and Graham, 1907), I, 127.
2. George Matheson, "O Love That Wilt Not Let Me Go."
3. John Greenleaf Whittier, "To Paths Unknown."

VII. Living On
1. Clarence E. Macartney, *Macartney's Illustrations* (New York and Nashville: Abingdon Press, 1945), pp. 179-80.
2. John Greenleaf Whittier, "The Friend's Burial."
3. Henry W. Longfellow, "Resignation."

VIII. Never Alone
1. William L. Stidger, *More Sermons in Stories* (New York and Nashville: Abingdon-Cokesbury Press, 1944), p. 132.
2. William L. Stidger, *Sermon Nuggets in Stories* (New York and Nashville: Abingdon Press, 1946), pp. 66-67.
3. Anonymous.

IX. Moving Toward the Fold
1. James Montgomery, "At Home in Heaven."
2. Frederick B. Speakman, *The Salty Tang* (Westwood, New Jersey: Fleming H. Revell Company, 1954), p. 42.
3. Anonymous.

X. The Darkened Doorway
1. William L. Stidger, *Sermon Stories of Faith and Hope* (New York and Nashville: Abingdon Press, 1948), pp. 127-28.
2. John Oxenham, "God's To-morrow," Charles L. Wallis, *op. cit.,* p. 250.

XI. By My Side
1. Robert Browning, "Paracelsus."

XII. Not to Be Feared
1. Catherine Marshall, *A Man Called Peter* (New York, London, and Toronto: McGraw-Hill Book Company, Inc., 1951), p. 261.
2. Alfred Lord Tennyson, "Crossing the Bar."

XIII. The First Five Minutes
1. William N. Clarke in John James MacNeill, *Many Mansions* (New York: George H. Doran Company, 1926), p. 29.
2. Emily Brontë, "Last Lines."

XIV. Only a Line

1. Leslie D. Weatherhead, *The Transforming Friendship* (Abingdon Press: New York and Nashville, 1931), p. 157.

2. Frank E. Graeff, "Does Jesus Care," Copyright 1901, Renewal, 1929. The Rodeheaver Co., Owner. All Rights Reserved.

3. *The Ministers Manual*, 1951, p. 171.

4. John Greenleaf Whittier, from "Snow-Bound."

XV. On Being Ready

1. Archer Wallace, *The Autograph of God* (New York: The Macmillan Company, 1952), p. 145.

2. William D. Longstaff, "Take Time to Be Holy."

3. Fanny J. Crosby, "Saved by Grace."

XVI. My Shepherd

1. Frederick L. Hosmer, "Friends Beyond," Charles L. Willis, *op. cit.*, pp. 243-44.

XVII. On a Gray Day

1. Leslie D. Weatherhead, *That Immortal Sea* (New York and Nashville: Abingdon Press, 1953), p. 44.

2. Lowell R. Ditzen, *Personal Security Through Faith* (New York: Henry Holt and Company, 1954), pp. 226-27.

3. Miss M. E. Servoss, "He Will Hide Me."

XVIII. At Peace

1. Frederick B. Harris, *Spires of the Spirit* (New York and Nashville: Abingdon Press, 1952), p. 50.

2. Anonymous, Murdock Mackinnon, *The Imprisoned Splendour* (London: H. R. Allenson, Publishers), p. 128.

3. G. A. Studdert-Kennedy, "Peace and Joy" from "The Suffering God," *The Unutterable Beauty, op. cit.*, p. 4.

XIX. Preparing for Glory

1. James Montgomery, "The Earth Is Full of God's Goodness."

2. Elizabeth B. Browning, from "Work."

XX. The Great Divide

1. Ralph Sockman in Alton Motter, ed., *Great Preaching Today* (New York: Harper and Brothers, 1955), p. 218.

2. Charlotte Elliott, "Just As I Am."

3. Robert Service, "The Land of Beyond," *Rhymes of a Rolling Stone* (New York: Dodd, Mead and Company, 1914), p. 16. Reprinted

123

by permission of Ryerson Press and of Dodd, Mead & Company from *The Collected Poems of Robert Service.* Copyright © 1912, 1940, by Robert Service.

XXI. Full of the Right Things
1. Grace N. Crowell, "Prayer at the Feet of Mountains," *Light of the Years* (New York and London: Harper and Brothers, 1936), p. 45.

XXII. The Path
1. H. V. Larcombe in A. Gordon Nasby, *op. cit.*, p. 377.
2. Giles Fletcher, Jr., "The Excellency of Christ," James Dalton Morrison, ed., *Masterpieces of Religious Verse* (New York and London: Harper and Brothers, 1948), p. 137.

XXIII. Completing Unfinished Plans
1. Lewis L. Dunnington, *Keys to Richer Living* (New York: The Macmillan Company, 1952), p. 52.
2. John Greenleaf Whittier, from "To My Friend on the Death of His Sister."

XXIV. Behold the Stars
1. Leslie D. Weatherhead.
2. R. Sirhowy Jones in A. Gordon Nasby, *op. cit.*, p. 41.
3. Quoted in William Henry Furness, "Evening Hymn," Burton E. Stevenson, *op. cit.*, p. 2969.

XXV. Listening for His Footstep
1. Quoted in *The Ministers Manual*, 1952, p. 147.
2. William Wordsworth, "The Excursion," Book VII.
3. George Eliot, "Making Life Worth While."

XXVI. Drawing Back the Curtain
1. Anonymous.
2. Anna Blake Mazquida, *Good Housekeeping.* Reprinted by permission of *Good Housekeeping.*

XXVII. The Master's Garden
1. Ralph Connor (Charles William Gordon), *The Sky Pilot* (Chicago, New York and Toronto: Fleming H. Revell Company, 1899), pp. 177-179.

2. Jane Eliza Leeson, "Gracious Saviour, Gentle Shepherd."

XXVIII. Rungs unto Heaven
1. James Russell Lowell, "On the Death of a Friend's Child."
2. Joshiah G. Holland, "Gradatim," James D. Morrison, *op. cit.,* p. 443.